What's In a Family Name

WHAT'S IN A FAMILY NAME

A Southern Family History Becomes a Gothic Mystery

STEVE SUITTS

BLACK BELT PRESS

MONTGOMERY

Black Belt Press
105 S. Court Street
Montgomery, AL 36104
www.foranewsouth.com

Cataloging-in-Publication Data

ISBN 978-1-961938-25-0

Design by Randall Williams

Printed in the United States of America

BLACK BELT PRESS • MONTGOMERY

The Black Belt, defined by its dark, rich soil, stretches across central Alabama. It was the heart of the cotton belt. It was and is a place of great beauty, of extreme wealth and grinding poverty, of pain and joy. Here we take our stand, listening to the past, looking to the future.

In memory of Tommy,
my big brother always

Deny thy father and refuse thy name…
Nor arm nor face nor any other part
Belonging to a man. O be some other name.
— ROMEO AND JULIET

"And so, in a sense, the affair, no matter what happens out there tonight, will still be in the family; the skeleton (if it be a skeleton) still in the closet."
— ABSALOM ABSALOM

"If it ain't complicated it don't matter whether it works or not because if it ain't complicated enough it ain't right."
— THE TOWN

"I reckon anybody named for Colonel Sartoris in this country can't help but tell the truth, can they?"
— "BARN BURNING"

"My first recollection of the name was, no outsider seemed able to pronounce it from reading it…"
— WILLIAM FAULKNER TO MALCOLM COWLEY, EXPLAINING THE INSERT OF "U" INTO HIS SURNAME

Contents

Introduction: 'I Can't Stop Loving You' / ix

1 GTT—'Gone To Texas' / 3

2 'Cutting Words' / 8

3 Until Death Do Us Part / 12

4 'When the Roll Is Called Up Yonder' / 20

5 'Delayed Birth . . .' / 24

6 May All Your Troubles Be 'Little Ones' / 28

7 Mr. Suitts Appears / 39

8 Things Others Would Forget / 45

9 When That Name Had Only One 'T' / 51

10 'Perished as Though They Had Never Been' / 57

11 Corrigendum / 63

12 Genealogical Epilogue: Scalawag James Monroe Blackwell / 64

Acknowledgments / 82

Index / 85

Lauderdale
• **Florence**
Athens
• Limestone
Madison
Jackson

Colbert

• **Decatur**
Lawrence
Morgan
Marshall
DeKalb

Franklin

Haleyville • • **Littleville**
Marion
Winston
Cullman
• **Boaz**
Cherokee

Double Springs
Jasper
• Walker
Blount
Etowah

Lamar
Fayette
Jefferson
•
Birmingham
St Clair
Calhoun
Cleburne

Pickens
Tuscaloosa
Shelby
Talladega
Clay
Randolph

Greene
Hale
Bibb
Chilton
Coosa
Tallapoosa
Chambers

Sumter
Perry
Autauga
Elmore
Lee

Marengo
Dallas
Montgomery
Macon
Russell

Choctaw
Wilcox
Lowndes
Bullock

Clarke
Butler
Crenshaw
Pike
Barbour

Washington
Monroe
Conecuh
Coffee
Dale
Henry

Escambia
Covington
Geneva
Houston

Mobile
Baldwin

RELEVANT ALABAMA LOCATIONS

Introduction

'I Can't Stop Loving You'

I never liked my father, and I am not sure I ever loved him. I am sure many other children have had a worse parent, but I realized early in my life that Troy Suitts was quick to anger, even quicker to act on his rage, and largely uninterested in me and my brother, Tommy. My first memory of Dad is around the age of four or five, and it involves his instructing me to repeat the words "real live rabbits" to friends and strangers alike. The phrase came out of my mouth as "will wive wabbits." My inability to pronounce an "r" was apparently all the funnier because I sounded like Elmer Fudd, the popular, buffoonish character who was always chasing "wabbits" in the cartoons at the movies in the 1940s and '50s. There are photographs of Dad and me at earlier ages, but I have no picture of him in my mind's eye before my "wabbit" talks.

Dad wasn't around our house much when I was growing up in Haleyville, Alabama, even before my mother divorced him in 1958 "on account of cruelty," as the decree tactfully stated. My only recall of family travel beyond visiting relatives was a day trip to Shiloh Battlefield, where in 1862 almost twenty-four thousand soldiers died, more casualties than in all of America's previous wars combined. After Tommy and I climbed cannon ball mounts, replayed the War, and were treated to snazzy sunglasses and Civil War caps (his gray, mine blue), Mom told us that my father would be leaving our apartment in Haleyville's federal housing project. On the way home, we visited nearby Pickwick Dam, which Mom's father had helped build during the New Deal. She took a picture of Troy and his boys in the parking lot. No one was happy.

From left, Tommy, Troy, and Steve Suitts at Pickwick Dam.

Troy never paid child support, in part because he had trouble holding down a job. He tried several—working on the railroad, selling insurance, driving a truck, building roads, serving as a police officer, and others. He particularly liked selling insurance since it let him sit and talk leisurely with folks; to my later surprise, he spent as much time sitting on the porches of blacks as he did on those of whites. Even today a few African American women in Haleyville remember him flirting with them as young girls and having their daddies take him home since he was too drunk to drive.

I am not sure when Dad became an alcoholic, but it was early in my life. I figured out afterwards why he spent so much time at the American Legion Hall: men congregated there in legally dry Winston County to share illegal moonshine or whiskey. It was not rare for Mom to get a call to come pick up Troy after he passed out at the Legion Hall, a restaurant parking lot, or someone's house. She often had to walk to the spot since he would have driven our car.

After Mom moved us to a smaller apartment in the town's segregated housing project, Troy tried often to break into our house. I have a clear memory of country singer Don Gibson's original version of "I Can't Stop Loving You" blasting from Dad's car radio as I watched him pull out heavy iron chains from the trunk. Mom sent Tommy and me upstairs. Slurred pleas, drunken yells, crashes of broken glass, and screams inevitably followed. The police would arrive, and Troy would be hauled away to sober up and get a warning.

Mom sought counsel and assistance from her pastor at the Haleyville Church of Christ, but after listening to her story he said she should never have divorced Troy. The Bible, he insisted, commanded her to submit to her husband in all matter and circumstances. Mom never went back to the church, although she continued to send Tommy and me on Sundays.

It got so bad that Mom took Tommy and me to stay with her brother Billy, who was stationed at Fort Campbell, Kentucky. She thought a military base would be a safe harbor. And it was. She did let Dad visit us there once. He arrived on a snowy Monday, took Tommy and me for breakfast to a restaurant that was closing early due to weather, and dropped us off downhill from the school so he could quickly leave town before the roads became impassable. The school was closed, and no one was there. Tommy and I walked the three miles back, and I got a frightful case of frostbite.

We went back to Haleyville after a semester since Uncle Billy's house was too small for two families, and Mom couldn't find steady work near the base. After we returned, the break-ins resumed with the same threatening routine. Dad would not—or could not—live up to Gibson's lyrics: "I can't stop wanting you, it's useless to say / So I'll just live my life in dreams of yesterday." It was more like nightmares of tonight. Finally in the fall of 1960, Mom found a dollar-an-hour job at Woolworth's five and dime in Florence, Alabama, fifty miles north on the Tennessee River, and we moved to a boardinghouse within easy walking distance of her job and our new school. We were without a car, and Mom's brother-in-law, Pike, moved us and our worldly belongings in his pickup truck.

Two weeks before we left Haleyville for good, its city council confirmed the appointment of Troy Suitts as one of the town's policemen. I suppose he was more qualified than most in his knowledge of police cars, the town's police station, and the local practice of not arresting or preventing drunken ex-husbands from breaking into the homes of their children and beating their ex-wives.

THESE MEMORIES BEGIN WHERE this book's story about the extra "t" in my surname ends. I'm including them to reveal not so much the story's aftermath as my own personal reckoning. Given these recollections, why did I undertake decades of genealogical research about my father's family but not about my mother's? My tenacious, amazing mother and her relatives, especially her parents, cared for me throughout my youth. They made me feel safe, capable, and loved as a child. Later, I recorded Mom's stories about her family's history handed down across generations, and she diligently sought out information about her ancestors that I requested but only stored away.

Why? The reasons surprise me. Yes, I had a nagging need to discover how I came by my oddly spelled surname since it acts like a crest of self-identity. But I reckon now that I had another need—to search for an explanatory backstory that might mitigate those raw, desperate times in my youth when I reviled my father.

Don't get me wrong. I had some pleasant moments with Dad and his side of the family. Growing up, I enjoyed playing with my cousins Sherman, Mark, and Danny, although I saw them randomly. I thought Wesley Steele, my father's uncle, was a wickedly funny storyteller. Based on her remembrances, my mother admired Granny Steele, my father's grandmother. And before I embarked on this book, as the Epilogue shows, I rejoiced in discovering documents confirming that my father's ancestors in north Alabama fought for the Union in the Civil War and afterwards supported Southern Reconstruction.

In addition, Dad's rage and alcoholism waned over the decades, especially after his eyesight diminished, and afterwards being with him did not always mean trouble. But we were never able to construct a meaningful relationship. It remained rocky, oscillating across my adult years from open hostility to polite indifference, until the day he died.

After we settled safely in Florence, despite the brutality she had suffered at his hands, Mom urged me several times to understand that I did not have to like my father in order to love my father. Over time I grasped more fully her meaning, and, as I researched and wrote this book, her insight guided me to a new appreciation for how lineage and circumstances may have helped to shape Troy Suitts and his character. But as much as I might wish for a different conclusion, the story I tell cannot change the aftermath nor does it engender in me a change of heart, engorged as it is now with genuine pity for the flawed man whose surname I share.

Steve Suitts
Atlanta, Georgia

What's In a Family Name

SUITTS FAMILY TREE

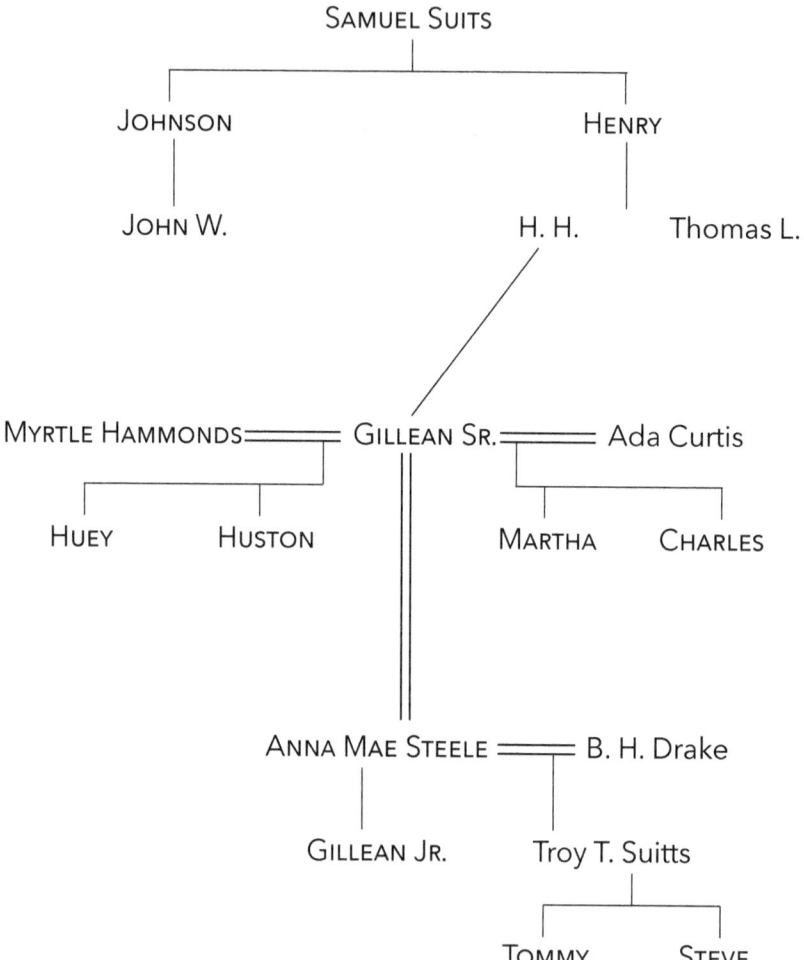

1

GTT–'Gone To Texas'

M y family name has two "t"s although it is pronounced as if it has only one—suits—like what a lawyer files in court or what men once wore to church as their Sunday best. For most of my life it has been mispronounced on both sides of the Mason-Dixon Line because the extra "t" seemingly makes no sense. Often it has been expressed as "suites," as if my family origins were derived from a Hilton Hotel room with a sitting area. As an antidote to my injured familial pride, I have relished for more than three decades the opportunity to tell the story about how I came by the extra letter in my surname.

My paternal grandmother, Anna Mae Steele, born a twin with her brother Willie in 1899, came of age in Winston County, Alabama, a densely forested county with a ragged, soil-poor terrain, which is known in Alabama history as the "Free State of Winston." Once the American Civil War broke out, many of Winston's white residents met and decided not to fight for the Confederacy to help it maintain slavery. Like Andrew Jackson, they did not believe the Constitution permitted secession, and, except for seventeen local families, none were enslavers.

Many families, including Anna's own ancestors, actively supported the Union during the War. A plurality if not a majority of Winston County's draft-eligible men enlisted and fought in the Union Army, mostly in the First Alabama Cavalry USA, which helped General William Tecumseh Sherman plunder the Deep South states into submission. Others in Winston and surrounding counties evaded Confederate conscription and aided Northern troops. Anna's maternal grandfather, James Monroe Blackwell,

3

Richard A. Steele, First Alabama Cavalry USA Records.

too old to fight, was jailed more than once by Confederate soldiers who threated to kill him because he was known as a "Union Tory" supporting Lincoln's war. In defiance, Blackwell publicly announced that he had named his youngest son Abraham Lincoln Blackwell.* He also provided Union soldiers with information and supplies and helped a wounded Union soldier return safely to his unit.

Richard Andrew Steele, Anna's paternal great-grandfather, volunteered at age fifty as a blacksmith for the Union's First Alabama Cavalry as soon as it was formed. Afterwards he may have been in league with the six Union-loyal sons of John Solomon Curtis who banded together in a series of revenge killings against the Confederates they believed were responsible for murdering three of their brothers, including Pinkney "Pink" Curtis. When slain, Pink was Winston's duly elected, pro-Union probate judge who, like all nine brothers, followed his father's dying wish to defy Alabama's Confederate state government and remain loyal to the Union.

I didn't know all this family history when I first patched together the story about my surname, and my grandmother Anna never spoke to me about it, although her older brother, Wesley, did talk occasionally about how our family was Republican and included some Native American lineage. (Richard's wife, Celie, was Cherokee and, according to a family Bible, "was buried with her pure china cup, saucer, and plate, also her beaded belt, headband, moccasins that she made for herself.") As a young man, I knew enough to realize my own Southern heritage was unique. As a white boy born in 1949 in the heart of Dixie, ruled by segregationist Democrats, one side of my family was Republican and had remained so since the Civil War.

My grandmother came of age living with her parents, Andrew Thomas and Malvina Christine Steele, in Littleville, just outside of Haleyville (then a town of 1,111) on the road to Winston's county seat, Double Springs (then a town of 1,571). By the time I came along, her community was better known as Needmore—for self-evident reasons, according to my

---

* See Chapter 12 for the full story in "Genealogical Epilogue: Scalawag James Monroe Blackwell."

grandmother's older brother, Wesley. Some local residents called Wes its unofficial mayor; befitting this role, he used to wear stiff overalls with a pressed white shirt and tie.

The family story begins there around 1917 or 1918 when Anna was about eighteen and fell in love with Gillean Lafayette Suits (one "t"), a county deputy sheriff. "He was so handsome in his uniform," my grandmother remembered more than sixty-five years later.

Unfortunately, Gillean was already engaged to the daughter of the county's most powerful man, John Solomon Curtis, Winston's probate judge, who was named after his patriarchal grandfather and held the same office as his Civil War uncle, Pink Curtis. Members of the Curtis clan had held virtually every elected public office in the county, and the latest Judge John S. Curtis had retained his post since 1904.

As the United States entered World War I, love and romance proved more powerful than ancient family loyalties, marital engagements, patriotism, and political power. "Mr. Suitts said his mother would die if he went to war," my grandmother told me. She always called him Mr. Suitts, perhaps because he was older than her (she said eighteen years older, but actually eleven). The two lovers followed an Alabama tradition from early territorial days when a couple or family abandoned their cabin in the dark of night, leaving behind debts or other troubles and a paint-marked message on the front door: "GTT"— Gone to Texas. In this case, Anna and Gillean fled, telling hardly anyone where they were going.

They escaped to Ennis, Texas, a small town about forty miles east of Dallas where the Houston & Texas Central Railway had a repair depot for its trains. Gillean added an extra "t" to his last name to camouflage his whereabouts and found a job as an accountant in the local railroad office. The couple settled into a home about a mile away from the railroad station, and by early 1920 they had their first child, my uncle Gillean Lafayette Suitts Jr. Within a year, however, Mr. Suitts began suffering severe headaches and only a few months later he died of a brain hemorrhage. Afterwards, with the assistance of the railroad company, Anna Suitts returned to her parents' home in Littleville with little Gillean in tow. She was also pregnant with her second child, my father.

So, I have two "t"s in my surname because my grandparents fell in love and eloped to Texas! To my profound surprise, the extra "t" had been enough of a veil to keep the couple from being discovered by Judge Curtis and others from Winston County.

The only problem with this story is that almost all of it is a lie. The only part that my grandmother—with the help of her mother—did not fabricate was that she and Gillean ran away to Texas together and he died there. The real story, the truth of the matter that I have pieced together only in recent years, is far stranger than Anna's boy-meets-girl fictional love story and my romantic tale of how I got my family name.

2

'Cutting Words'

Gillean Suits's family had trouble nailing down the spelling of their surname long before he met Anna Mae Steele. Was it singular, Suit, or plural, Suits? As far back as the 1700s, Gillean's forebearers were identified in surviving records as both. Anyone involved in genealogical research knows it was customary across the nation's first three centuries that free people spelled and pronounced names in numerous, often unusual ways. It was an oral culture in which few could read or write, and, as the new nation embodied more people of diverse cultures, languages, and accents, people's names were often written down according to what was heard more than said or written.

The name-spelling remained fluid as members of the Suits clan migrated from Maryland to North Carolina, Georgia, and finally to east Tennessee where Gillean's grandfather settled around Ducktown, about five miles from where the latter states join. Henry Suits had lived in all three states, farming on unclaimed lands for his father and later with his own growing family until he became an experienced collier working around local ore and copper mines. In the late 1850s, J. R. Phillips, an ambitious, energetic young man, hired Suits to make charcoal, which Phillips sold to the local Congdon Mines.

The two men worked together in the vicinity of Ducktown making charcoal and loading it on wagons day and night. Phillips was eager to master the art of charcoal-making and stayed throughout the night because "Suits was afraid to stay alone at night," Phillips remembered in his memoir, while "I was afraid of nothing." The men soon quarreled, and Phillips ran Suits out of the coal yard until the older man returned, apologized, and was rehired—but only as a part time helper, not a partner.

Shortly before the outbreak of the Civil War, Phillips decided to find new opportunities and new land in what he called the "west." He traveled on foot with his wife into Alabama and settled originally in Winston County, close to what would become Haleyville. Phillips claimed cheap land from the federal government's land office and built a modest cabin. A few months later, one of his Tennessee neighbors showed up. It was John W. Suits, Henry's nephew. John was accompanied by his wife, child, and his wife's grown sister, all of whom Phillips welcomed into the one-room cabin, no larger than eighteen by sixteen feet, where he and his wife lived.

According to Phillips, John Suits was amiable and helpful but lacked energy and independence. Suits told Phillips: "Where you go, I will go; where you locate, I locate." Phillips later remembered, "John was a good worker but would give out before night some days when we were doing hard work." He considered Suits a "much older man" because of his lack of stamina and his unkempt bearded face. Records show that Suits was small in stature but only four years older than Phillips.

Phillips also remembered that "Mrs. Suits was a large, white-eyed woman, good natured and kind but very high tempered. She was very quarrelsome with her husband, who being a good natured man, took it

John R. Phillips

all. I took up for him, then she and I quarreled daily. She did not care what she said and would laugh at my cutting words."

When Phillips moved a short distance across the county line into Marion County for better soil, Suits and his family followed. The two men lived near each other and farmed together until the start of the Civil War. Both enlisted in the First Alabama Cavalry USA to fight for the Union, but not at the same time. They also did not serve in the same unit. Suits spent a good part of his enlistment in Winston and Marion counties attempting to recruit north Alabama men to join the Union Army, and, when the War closed, he stayed near Decatur, Alabama, on the Tennessee River where he was stationed. Phillips returned to Marion County, where he became a successful local merchant. He helped to establish the local public school that his Bear Creek community named for him.

Beginning in the late 1870s, John Suits received a monthly war pension from the federal government for serving in the Union Army. (Most Confederate veterans were eligible for a smaller state pension but at that time only if they were indigent or disabled.) Later, Suits claimed an increased federal pension due to a leg injured while traveling as a soldier from Nashville to Decatur at the end of the War. Following his death in 1904, his wife, Mary, received a widow's pension until 1911 when a federal examiner questioned whether she had been lawfully married to John before his first wife died in childbirth. There was no available documentary evidence of the marriage, but a distant cousin, intriguingly named Steve Suits, helped save Mary's pension by recalling in an affidavit that John's first wife was dead when Mary and John married at a public ceremony.

THE MEN OF GILLEAN Suits's extended family fought on different sides of the Civil War. John's younger brother, Ransom Suits, fought for the Confederate's 19th Tennessee Infantry and his cousin, Johnston Suits, was killed while serving as a Confederate private in the 6th Alabama Infantry. Another cousin, Ralph Suits, was killed as a Union soldier in Arkansas.

Gillean's grandfather, Henry, the collier, was eligible to be drafted into either the Confederate or Union armies, but he evaded both sides while remaining in eastern Tennessee. Gillean's father, Henry Huston—H. H.,

John W. Suits's US Military Pension.

as he became known—was born after the War in 1866 and grew up in eastern Tennessee while his father continued working around mines and quarries. H. H. married Nancy Gillean, the daughter of a deceased local farmer, in August 1887 when he was twenty-one and she was twenty-seven. Five and a half months later, Gillean Huey Suits[*] was born in Birmingham, Alabama, where his parents had recently moved seeking a new life in the South's emerging industrial core.

---

[*] During his lifetime, Gillean used and others referred to him by different names and various spellings of his name. The family tree on page 2 lists him as simply "Gillean Sr." and the index lists his various names in the text under "Suit or Suits, Gillean."

3

Until Death Do Us Part

L ittle is known about Gillean as a boy, except that he attended school and lived with his parents as an only child, although his parents lost another in childbirth. H. H. Suit was identified in the 1900 census as a self-employed carpenter who repaired rail cars in the Birmingham area. Gillean was twelve.

On June 27, 1909, Gillean married Myrtle Hammonds, a petite red-headed daughter of a puddler who worked in Birmingham's iron furnaces. The couple "performed the rite of matrimony," in the isolated Bamford community, a mining area about twenty miles south of Birmingham. Gillean was twenty-one, and Myrtle was fifteen. The newlyweds married in Bamford probably because it was in Shelby County, not Birmingham's Jefferson County where they could not get hitched. Alabama law required a marriage affidavit affirming that the bride was eighteen years or older and a marriage bond of two hundred dollars to be forfeited to the state in the event an under-age marriage was undertaken without her parents' permission. Neither affidavit nor bond were filed with the marriage license.

A Shelby County miner, who served as both a local minister and a justice of the peace, married the couple. He was also a perennial Republican office-seeker, then running for the state legislature. The probate judge who enrolled the marriage license in the county books was also a Republican who once represented Shelby County in the state legislature. Gillean's own political affiliation at that time is unknown, but he clearly understood Alabama politics enough to know the right place to marry. In 1909, the tiny number of Republican local officials across Alabama did not question one another about whether the Democratic-dominated legislature's laws requiring forms and bonds were followed to a "t," especially when receiving a fee for performing and recording a marriage. As it happens, the obliging minister-JP was elected to the state legislature in 1910 as one of only four Republican members, including another from Winston County.

Nine months later, on March 26, 1910, Myrtle Suit gave birth to her first child, Huey, near Winston County's Double Springs. It's unclear when the couple moved there or if Gillean attended his son's birth. A census taker recorded on April 15 of that year that Gillean was employed repairing cars in Birmingham and living with his mother's relatives next door to his own parents. Gillean probably moved his family to the land in Winston County that his father, H. H., purchased from the federal land office in 1898 following John W. Suits's move to Alabama. It was also the place where Myrtle and Gillean's second child, diplomatically named Huston, was born fifteen days before Christmas in 1911.

By 1913, Gillean had started a car service in Double Springs, providing

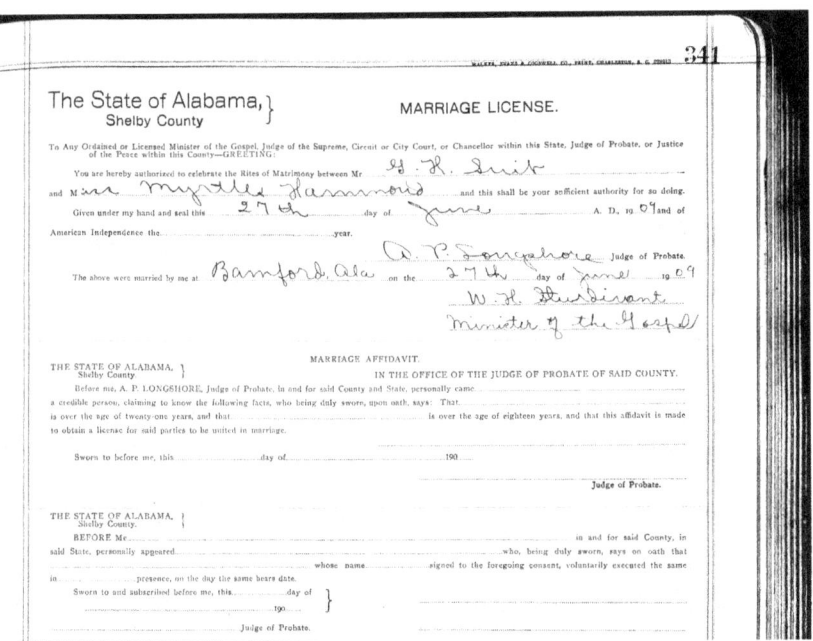

Gillean Suit's first marriage certificate.

county residents with a new form of transportation at a time when the automobile was only beginning to appear on Alabama roads from Northern factories. A new passenger train now ran through Haleyville, but its daily service bypassed almost all of Winston County. The train was the only public means of transporting people southward to Jasper in adjoining Walker County or to Birmingham and northward to the Tennessee Valley, northeastern Mississippi, and beyond. Apart from hitchhiking, Gillean's car service was the only public means for people to go back and forth to Haleyville and Double Springs.

Automobiles were a new, faster way to travel on dirt roads although wagons and horseback remained the primary means of transport in Alabama, and some local folks remained baffled and skeptical of the machine. My maternal grandfather, who decades later became a railroad man in Haleyville, remembered seeing a farmer hitch a team of mules to the rear of a Model-T Ford before he cranked it. The neighbor didn't trust the car to stop once the engine started and moved forward. But the local newspaper editor in Double Springs was a true believer in the new means of progress. "Gillian Suits starts this morning for Birmingham," he wrote in May 1913. "He will go through in his car."

A month later, the *Winston Herald* editor again wrote that "Gillian Suits has purchased another fine automobile and will put both of his machines on the route to Haleyville. We understand he will inaugurate an every-other-day schedule, which will be a great convenience to our people, as it will give the traveling public quick service to the railroad."

As Gillean established himself as an entrepreneur, his marriage fell apart. No record of his divorce has been found, and it is likely there was none. In Alabama, a divorce decree was hard to obtain, expensive, and took years to finalize. Many couples followed the example of Myrtle's own mother when she separated from her husband and afterwards identified herself as a widow. Records do show that on Valentine's Day, 1914, Myrtle Suit married S. E. Dodson in a ceremony conducted by the pastor of Birmingham's Third Presbyterian Church after Dodson completed the necessary forms at the Jefferson County Courthouse, including filing an age affidavit and a marriage bond.

There is also no available information as to why the young couple went their separate ways, but everything strongly indicates it was because of Gillean's infidelity. The records in the probate judge's office evidence that on May 16, three months after Myrtle's new marriage, Dr. Thomas Drake of Double Springs delivered an unnamed child, later christened Martha Jane Suits, as the newborn of Ada Curtis and "G. H. Soots." Ada was the daughter of Probate Judge John S. Curtis. The entry in the county's *Register of Births* reflects the phonetics of Gillean's surname, but it seems strange that Judge Curtis's own staff would have badly misspelled the name of someone who was already well known in the local community as a businessman. In retrospect, it is quite possible the spelling of Gillean's surname was deliberately mangled in case Judge Curtis did not want his office's records to accurately identify the father of his unmarried daughter's child.

That option was eliminated on July 30, sixty-six days after Ada gave birth to Martha Jane. In a "shotgun wedding," Judge Curtis married his twenty-four-year-old daughter to twenty-six-year-old Gillean in a civil ceremony without named witnesses. The location is unknown. The official record also failed to include customary information about the age, race, religion, characteristics, or occupation of the couple, nor did the Judge complete the form showing whether the marriage was performed with the consent of the parents [see next page]. Apparently, the less written the better—an attitude replicated in the local newspapers, where the marriage of the county's leading public official's daughter went without notice, recognition, or comment.

Even before the birth of Judge Curtis's grandchild, Gillean's mother, Nancy "Tiny" Suits, had moved to Winston County and was overseeing the construction of a new house that would become home for her only son and his family near where Gillean and Myrtle previously lived. As Christmas approached in 1915, Ada and Gillean had a second child, Charles, who, like his older sister, was named only after the birth was recorded in a handwritten notation in the probate judge's books. This time the official record indicated the correct spelling of the father's name and included an accurate notation that Gillean was in his second marriage and was now the father of four children (by two marriages).

535

MARRIAGE RECORD

WINSTON COUNTY, ALABAMA.

Mr. .... and M ....

THE STATE OF ALABAMA, WINSTON COUNTY.

To any Licensed Minister of the Gospel, or Judge of the Supreme or Circuit Courts or Chancellor within this State,
or Judge of Probate or Justice of the Peace within this County—GREETING:

You are hereby authorized to celebrate the RITE OF MATRIMONY between Mr. *G. H. Suits*

and M .. *i.e* *Ada Curtis* ...., and this shall be your sufficient authority for so doing.

Given under my hand this *3.0* day of *July* ......, 191 *4* .... *John O Curtis*, Judge of Probate.

THE STATE OF ALABAMA, WINSTON COUNTY.

This certifies that I have solemnized marriage between Mr. *G H Suits* ....and M .. *i.e* *Ada Curtis*

according to law, at.... *Double Spring*..in said County and State, on this *3 0* day of *July* ......, 191 *4*

John O Curtis

Probate Judge

THE STATE OF ALABAMA, WINSTON COUNTY.

KNOW ALL MEN BY THESE PRESENTS, That we, ... are held and firmly bound unto the State of Alabama in the penal sum of Two Hundred Dollars, for the payment of which, well and truly to be made, we bind ourselves and every one of our heirs, executors, and administrators, jointly and severally, firmly by these presents.

Sealed with our seals and dated the .... day of .... A. D. One Thousand Nine Hundred and ....

The CONDITION OF THE ABOVE OBLIGATION IS SUCH, That whereas, the above bound, ... has obtained license to marry and be joined in the Bonds of Matrimony with ....; Now, if there be no lawful cause why such marriage should not be celebrated, then this obligation to be void; otherwise to remain in full force and effect.

.... (L. S.)

.... (L. S.)

.... (L. S.)

Taken and approved the .... day of .... 191 .... Judge of Probate.

RECORD AS TO AGES OF PARTIES, CONSENT OF PARENT OR GUARDIAN, ETC.

Age of Man	Is there any blood relationship betwixt the parties, and if so what? ....
Age of Woman	
Color of Man	Religious belief of Man ....
Color of Woman	Religious belief of Woman ....
Height of Man	Residence of Man ....
Height of Woman	Residence of Woman ....
Weight of Man	Remarks: ....
Weight of Woman	
Nativity of Man	
Nativity of Woman	
Occupation of Man	
Occupation of Woman	
Number Marriage of Man	
Number Marriage of Woman	

69176—Winston Co., Ala.

Gillean H. Suits's & Ada Curtis's marriage certificate.

Whatever his interests and motives in romancing the probate judge's daughter, Gillean seemed to prosper as Judge Curtis's son-in-law. He began hiring employees to work in his automobile business, including one of his cousins, Paul Herbert Gillean, as a mechanic. A year after his son Charles's birth, a Birmingham newspaper reported that "G. H. Suit of Haleyville" had joined two dozen other Alabama automotive businessmen enjoying first-class Pullman cars on a train trip to Toledo, Ohio. The owner of Over-land Motors was attempting to expand sales by entertaining auto salesmen and others with great "gobs" of amusement during five days of an all-expenses-paid visit to his factory. Apparently concerned that the Southern men "from the land of 'hot biscuits'" might not know how cold winters could get on the shore of Lake Erie, the auto manufacturer even provided his guests with heavy overcoats during their visit. Gillean had never been so far north of the Mason-Dixon Line.

LIFE BEGAN TO CHANGE after the United States entered World War I in April 1917. That June, Gillean had to register for possible military service in keeping with a new Selective Service Act requiring all males aged eighteen to thirty to get on the rolls for induction. He signed his registration card "Gillean Huey Suit"—not Suits. But answers on the form were even more telling. He claimed an exemption from military service due to his "support of two children" (not four) and his suffering from "rheumatism & heart trouble." Despite those claims, Gillean confusedly listed himself as being "single." Perhaps Ada and he were estranged by that time, or the answer could have been a Freudian slip reflecting his state of mind.

In early 1918, tragedy struck the Suits household. Not yet three years old, Gillean's son, Charles, died on February 9 after suffering from whooping cough and measles. He was buried the next day in the cemetery of Fairview Baptist Church near Double Springs. "Mrs. Suit's other child, a little girl also lies very low with the same disease, complicated with pneumonia," recounted the *Winston Herald*. A week later, the newspaper reported, "Died, last Sunday of whooping cough, Little Martha Suit, a small child of Mr. and Mrs. G. H. Suit, aged about four years." Martha was interred

Gravestones of Charles and Martha Suits.

beside her brother on a cemetery plot near the back road leading to the ancestral Curtis cemetery a few miles away.

Ten days later, in a peculiar coincidence, Myrtle Suits Dodson, the mother of Gillean's two older children, also died at the age of twenty-three in Birmingham, She was returned for burial to White County, Tennessee, where she was born.

Sometime during this period, Gillean encountered my grandmother, Anna Mae Steele, although there is no way to know exactly when they first met. She was living with her parents in Littleville along Byler Road, the oldest highway connecting north and south Alabama, that had led the first Suits into Alabama. For at least five years, Gillean regularly traveled through Littleville transporting local folks between Haleyville and Double Springs. Whatever the date of their initial meeting, this much is known. In 1918, Anna was nineteen, a slip of a child in appearance—less than four feet, ten inches tall and weighing less than a hundred pounds. Gillean was thirty years old and of medium height and weight. Little more than two months after the death of his two small children in Double Springs, Gillean and Anna had sex, leading nine months later to the birth of their first child in Texas.

The couple's act of conception may have been the beginning of their relationship, perhaps as Gillean sought comfort and release from his sorrows, or it may have been the consummation of a longer affair. There is no way to know. Also, there is no record or remembrance of exactly when in 1918 Anna and Gillean left Alabama for Texas. But the reasons they left are unmistakable. Gillean eloped with his new sweetheart for a fresh start, with a much younger woman and without the necessity of dealing with a grieving wife or the responsibilities that the death of two small children entails.

Leaving behind the probate judge's grief-stricken daughter, Gillean might have believed that the Curtis family and her friends would take care of Ada. They apparently were supportive. A local newspaper suggested late in 1918 that unmarried friends of "Mrs. Ada Suits" took her on an outing to the Natural Bridge, the county's primary tourist attraction. Ada also got a job as a clerk in a Haleyville general store, located in a new Curtis Building, ostensibly to occupy herself. But Ada was not the only person Gillean abandoned. He also left his two children, now without their mother, Myrtle, to become the responsibility of others. Myrtle's second husband refused or was incapable of raising Gillean's sons after her death. Within months after their mother's death, the two surviving Suits boys were split up. Gillean's mother and father began raising young Huey, and Myrtle's mother became young Huston's guardian. Their father never saw them again.

4

'When the Roll Is Called Up Yonder'

The first evidence that Gillean and Anna were settled in Texas is a document dated September 12, 1918. It is a draft registration card, which the government then required of all men up to age of forty-five. The registrant signed as "T. L. Suit" and is listed as "Thomas Lafayette Suit" living with his wife, "May Suit," in Ennis, Texas, on Sherman Street in a neighborhood of railroad men, teachers, and laborers. His occupation was carpenter at the Houston & Texas Central Railroad Company's (H&TC) repair shop. To improve his chances of avoiding the draft, Gillean claimed he was thirty-three, adding three years to his actual age, although it became an unnecessary dodge. Two months after he registered, hundreds gathered in downtown Ennis to celebrate the signing of the war-ending Armistice.

Gillean's alias was not a random choice. Thomas L. Suit was an uncle who in 1915 opened a blacksmith shop in the town of Heflin in east central Alabama, but by 1920 was a laborer in a cotton mill twenty-five miles away, across the state line in the town of Tallapoosa, Georgia. Married, Uncle Thomas Lafayette Suit had no children but now had a namesake.

On New Year's Day, 1919, Anna went into labor and at 3:50 a.m. the following morning delivered her first male child, not named on the birth certificate, with the assistance of Dr. Fred L. Story, a young physician who had recently moved to Ennis with his own Mexican bride. The father is listed as Thomas L. Suit, thirty-three, who along with his wife was reportedly born in Tennessee. "Annie May Sterns" is listed as the mother's maiden name, and she is described as a nineteen-year-old homemaker.

A year later, on January 30th, a female census taker (a job opened earlier to women due to wartime) recorded Tom L Suit, head of household, white, married, thirty-four, able to read and write, born in Tennessee, and working as a "car carpenter" in the railroad shop. Annie M. was listed as his wife, twenty-five, born in Tennessee. Their one-year-old son was identified as "Lafayette." My grandmother Anna, decades later, remembered Ennis as a prosperous time in her life—"We had a nice house, a car." If so, it was short-lived. By Christmas 1920, Gillean was seriously ill. On Boxing Day, Dr. J. W. Germany, the railroad company's doctor, examined Gillean and determined he had an abscess at the base of his brain—a brain tumor. The doctor "tried to convince Mr. Suitts to let him put him in the hospital in Dallas, but he refused," Anna recalled.

Downtown Ennis, Texas, on Armistice Day, 1918. (Library of Congress)

"I remember he came to me one day and put his arm around me," my grandmother continued. "'Honey,' he said, 'I don't think I'm gonna live. I hope I'm ready to die.'" A blood vessel broke "and he suffered." At 10 p.m. on January 11, 1921, at the couple's home at 1209 N. Sherman Street, Dr. Germany declared T. L. Suit, a.k.a. Gillean Huey Suit, dead.

His father, H. H. Suit, arrived in Ennis and with the assistance of the railroad company arranged to return his son's body to Birmingham for burial. H. H. did not reveal his son's real name and seemed unable to retrieve the year Gillean was born. "The railroad people were wonderful," Anna recalled decades afterwards. "Money! Money! Money!" she exclaimed. The H&TC apparently covered all outstanding financial obligations and

1921 death certificate of Gillean Suits, a.k.a. T. L. Suit.

paid for returning Anna and her son by rail to her parents' home outside of Haleyville.

Gillean's family was not so generous. Anna was shunned and quickly forgotten and never forgiven. She was not invited to attend Gillean's funeral and decades later she could not remember or, more likely, she never knew the cemetery where he was buried. "I was all shook up," she explained.

The family-produced obituary in the *Birmingham Post-Herald* on Monday, January 17, read:

> Funeral services of Gillean Suit, age 31, who died in Ennis, Texas, will be held this afternoon from the residence of his uncle, G. H. Gillean, at Pratt City. Interment in the Fraternal cemetery. Survived by wife and young son, and his parents, Mr. and Mrs. H. H. Suit of East Lake.

Although Gillean's family refused to identify Anna publicly as the widow and never communicated with her again, he had entrusted her with a dying man's wish. On his death bed, he asked that the song, "When the Roll Is Called Up Yonder," be sung at his funeral. It ends with the stanza: "When all of life is over, and our work on earth is done, and the roll is called up yonder, I'll be there." My grandmother, of course, had no idea whether the hymn was sung.

5

'Delayed Birth . . .'

Sitting in her house shortly before Christmas in 1984, almost sixty-four years to the day after Gillean received his deadly diagnosis, my grandmother was wishful about her first love and their brief time together in Texas: "I used to have a picture of him . . . he had this hat on . . . It was all blown up." She mused, "I should never have left Texas." But she did and, with her two-year-old son, Gillean Lafayette Jr., moved back to her parents' home in Littleville, where my father, Troy Turner, was later born.

As I listened to grandmother weave what I came to know as the facts and fictions of her life, I realized that after leaving Texas she spent the next seventy years going no further than thirty miles from the little community where we were sitting in 1984. I wondered then if she was embroidering her life story to substitute for what she had sought and missed, but I had no earthly idea until later just how much she had embellished. I did not discover until years after our interview that Gillean never added a "t" to his surname after they eloped. Similarly, I did not learn until decades later about his marriage to Judge Curtis's daughter and the death of their children within months of his leaving for Texas with my grandmother. And I had not yet found a copy of Gillean's death certificate—which in fact changed everything.

Human gestation can be measured by simple arithmetic, and the date on Gillean's death certificate seemed to establish that it was impossible that the man whose life I had been reassembling could be my grandfather! If grandmother was six months pregnant with my father when she left Texas, as she said in my interview, he would have been born in March or April of 1921. Even if she had been only one or two months pregnant when Gillean became ill, my father would have been born around August or September of 1921. My father always celebrated his birthday on July 4, 1922. If that date was correct, the math added up to one conclusion: there is no way Gillean could have procreated my father!

My search for the truth about how I got an extra letter in my family name was now a much bigger quest: simply put, who the hell really was my grandfather? Had there been a mistake in recording the year of my father's birth? Possibly, although every official document I had discovered in researching Gillean and Anna through Ancestry.com, FamilySearch.com, and other genealogical sources indicated that my father, Troy, was born on July 4, 1922. A couple of government records, including a reference to my parents' own marriage in 1947, indicated Troy's "Birth Date: abt 1923," but none suggested any date in 1921.

My father's birth certificate was nowhere to be found after he died in 2006. My brother Tommy and I failed to locate a copy among Troy's possessions, and my mother's old records drew a blank since she divorced him in 1958. So, I ordered a certified copy from the records division of the Alabama Department of Public Health—only to meet some surprising legal rigmarole.

Alabama law considers a birth certificate entirely confidential, strictly a private family matter unless the birth took place at least 125 years in the past—perhaps because paternity lawsuits seem to abound in Alabama. So, when I filed an online form to get my father's birth certificate, I had to provide my own birth certificate showing that I was Troy Suitts's son and fill in details about my father's date and place of birth as well as the names of his parents. My request was denied. I was told I had failed to correctly list his date of birth and the person listed as Troy's father on his birth certificate. I explained that I was not certain what the certificate showed for those facts. Too bad, the department representative responded—I would have to wait until 2047 when the record entered the public domain.

However, after I sent a long letter of protest to the department's general counsel explaining my problem, I received the birth certificate, except it was not really a birth certificate. It was called a "Delayed Birth Certificate" which documented information about my father's birth as an affidavit by my great-grandmother—Anna's mother, Malvina Steele. She swore it was true and accurate by making her "X" mark since she was unable to read or write. The form listed Troy's mother as "Annie Steele" and his father as "Gilland Suitts." It showed Troy's birth date as July 4, 1922. My grandmother also swore that Annie was "married to the father of this child" who was born outside Haleyville. The affidavit was dated more than twenty years after the fact, on February 20, 1943. I later figured out that the certificate must have been necessary more than two decades after my father's birth because he had been inducted into the army during World War II around the same time.

I KNEW THAT THE certificate's basic information had to be false, but those lies begged bigger questions. Why was there no original birth certificate? Why was there no attending physician or midwife at my father's birth who would have filed a regular birth certificate? Who could have fathered Anna's Alabama-born boy, my father, after she returned home in 1921? And why would Anna's mother lie, two decades after his birth, to hide the real father's identity?

The answers did not come right away, but they began to emerge after months of dead-end research when I finally stumbled onto an entry at *The Free State of Winston*, a website developed by the county's local historians and genealogists. In a listing of Winston County marriages from 1919 through 1923, the entry read:

557   Drake, B. H.   Suits, Annie Mae Steel   June 4, 1923

STOP! READ DIRECTIONS—FILL OUT BOTH SIDES

DELAYED CERTIFICATE OF BIRTH
STATE OF ALABAMA—BUREAU OF VITAL STATISTICS
STATE BOARD OF HEALTH

101-22-67619

File No. for State Registrar only
307

Reg. District No. _____ Certificate No. _____
To be filled out by local registrar

1. PLACE OF BIRTH:
County *Winston* 67
City or Town *Haleyville, Rural*
(If outside corporate limits of city or town write RURAL)

2. USUAL RESIDENCE OF MOTHER AT TIME OF THIS BIRTH:
State *Alabama*
County *Winston*
City or Town *Haleyville Rural*
(If outside corporate limits of city or town write RURAL)

3. FULL NAME OF CHILD AT TIME OF BIRTH:
Troy T. Suitts 320

4. Boy or Girl — *Boy*
5. Twin or triplet _____ If so—born 1st, 2d or 3d _____
7. Was mother married _____ of this child _____

Do not write below this line

Facts to be Supported by Documentary Evidence

Attention — Do not write in ruled boxes to right of this line

Form V. S. 4E—25M—12-42

	Baptismal Record	Family Bible	Insurance Policy	Affidavit	Attendant's Statement	Unsupported
Date of Birth				B	B	
Place of Birth				B	B	
Name of Father				B	B	
Name of Mother				B	B	

*Photostatic copies of evidence furnished responsible agencies on request at a nominal charge by the Bureau of Vital Statistics.
"A" record made before this person was 4 years old.
"B" record made after this person was 4 years old.

8. Date of birth of this child *July – 4 – 19 22*
(Month by name) (Day) (Year)

9. Full name of Father *Willard Suitts*
10. White or Colored race *w* 11. Age at time of this birth *Ala* yrs.
12. Birthplace *Ala*
(City or Town) (County) (State or foreign country)

13. Full name before marriage *Annie Steele*
14. White or Colored race *w* 15. Age at time of this birth *23* yrs.
16. Birthplace *Winston, Ala.*
(City or Town) (County) (State or foreign country)

17. CHILDREN BORN TO THIS MOTHER
(a) Children born alive and living at time of this birth, including this child *2*
(b) Previous children born alive but dead at time of this birth *0*
(c) Previous children born dead (stillborn) . . . *0*
Total number, including this birth, at time of this birth . . . . . *2* (Add a, b and c)

18. I hereby certify that I attended the birth of this child born alive on the date stated above.
Attendant's own signature _____ (Specify if M. D., midwife or other)
Date signed _____ (Month by name) (Day) 19 (Year)
Address _____

21. Signature of person registered: *Troy T. Suitts*
Note: Person registered should write own signature on line above exactly as used at present time.

20. Received.
Local or deputy registrar's own signature _____ JUN 8 1943 19 _____
Ralph W. Roberts

'5'

APPLICATION FOR DELAYED REGISTRATION
OF FACTS OF BIRTH

I, Malvina Steele
(Full name)*
, being first duly sworn on oath, testify that I am now 78 years of age and that the facts concerning my grandson set forth upon
(Son, daughter, ward, self)
the other side of this application are true and correct and that my present address is as follows:

Haleyville Alabama
(Street and number or rural route) (City or town) (State)

Signature* *Malvina her mark Steele*
Must agree exactly with that above

I certify that the above person appeared before me and testified as set forth above and affixed her
(His or her)
signature thereto and in my presence, this 20 day of February 19 43

Bernice Youngblood
(Signature of Notary Public)

Haleyville, Alabama
(Address of Notary Public)

Notary Public
Seal Here

Troy T. Suitts's birth affidavit.

6

May All Your Troubles Be 'Little Ones'

B. H. Drake—Burrus Hartwell Drake—was a pioneering merchant and landowner who helped develop Haleyville into the county's primary commercial center around the start of the twentieth century. His ancestors may have come to North America in the late 1600s as indentured servants. His great-grandfather, James Drake, was injured fighting for American Independence in North Carolina, although the family legend tells that his great-grandmother, named Hartwell, saved her husband's life by getting his anti-independence Tory captors "gloriously drunk" on apple brandy long enough for her neighbors to rescue Drake. Perhaps because of her clever spunk, both Burrus and his father carried her name.

Burrus was born three years after the end of the Civil War in Bartow County, Georgia, one of the sites northwest of Atlanta ravaged by Sherman's Army as Union troops marched to the sea, with the help of Winston County boys in the First Alabama Cavalry USA. Burrus's father, Hartwell Hughes, had lied about his age at sixteen so he could fight the British in the War of 1812. But Hartwell was sixty-two by the advent of the Civil War, too old for conscription. Married to a woman thirty-two years younger, Hartwell was nonetheless a vigorous, virile man. Burrus was conceived when his father was sixty-nine years old, only two years before the old man died from natural causes.

After Hartwell's death, Burrus's mother, Kisey Emeline, moved her family to Lawrence County, Alabama, during the 1870s as she traversed from one marriage to another. A genealogist of the Drake family has written that Emeline married five times and was so aged during the last exchange of vows that she had to be assisted to the altar.

In 1887, at age twenty, Burrus married Mary Melissa Curtis, the twenty-one-year-old daughter of William Verpo Curtis, another of Pink Curtis's brothers who supported the Union Army during the Civil War. Two years later, Burrus benefitted from his connection with the politically active Curtis family. He was appointed justice of the peace in a Winston County precinct around Gum Pond, an isolated community in the Sipsey River wilderness joining Lawrence and Winston counties. He maintained that post until he moved to Haleyville in 1897, eight years after the town incorporated.

By 1900, the Drake family had five children, ages one to eleven, and lived in Haleyville on the Byler Road, where Burrus was a bartender at Winston County's only drinking establishment, The Buckhorn Saloon. It advertised "all kinds of Fine Whiskies, such as: Green River, Planters' Rye, JackPot, Cascade 'Old' Edgemont, Nelson county, Ky. 'Rye,' Lincoln county Sobel, Log Cabin and Corn Whiskey of every description." It also supplied "Beers, Tobacco, and Cigars" and provided carry-outs: "Jug orders receive prompt attention." B. H. Drake, as Burrus had become known across the county, was in business with his wife's cousin, John Solomon Curtis—yes, a future probate judge and the father of Ada Curtis Suits.

As a Republican in Winston County, Curtis had effectively combined business and politics. He started as a merchant in the Haleyville area before it was incorporated. In 1886, his political connections got the local post office moved to inside his store, which likely increased his business. He was elected circuit court clerk in the same year and, while maintaining his businesses and serving occasionally as a special federal land commissioner, became one of the county's Republican leaders.

B. H. Drake followed Curtis's example. Described as early as 1901 as "one of Haleyville's best citizens" by the Double Springs weekly newspaper, Drake represented the county at the Republican state convention to nominate its statewide candidates, none of whom had a prayer of winning. He also was elected one of Haleyville's city aldermen. In 1903, as prohibition gained political momentum across rural Alabama, Curtis and Drake sold their liquor business. Curtis also may have needed the cash since a year earlier he had declared voluntary bankruptcy. But his political fortunes rose. He was elected probate judge and, while keeping his Haleyville business interests, moved his family, including daughter Ada, to Double Springs, the county seat.

As Judge Curtis became Winston County's chief political leader, B. H. Drake became one of its chief business leaders. He opened the Racket Store, a dry goods store in downtown Haleyville, in partnership with A. W. Moore. Soon Drake Mercantile Company erected its own huge general store and began expanding into other businesses. Drake purchased large parcels of land in and around Haleyville, including what became known as the Drake Farm in Littleville. By 1914, he was active in the Baptist Church, donating the land and assuring financing for the building of Haleyville's First Baptist Church. A year later, along with his oldest daughter, Ada, B. H. was a delegate to the state Baptist Convention.

By 1920, Drake was recognized across the state as a large, successful

Drake's Livery & Feeds Stables near Haleyville railroad. (Roy Keely Collection)

farmer and an influential businessman. While continuing his role as a city alderman and delegate to Republican state conventions, Drake became a stockholder and member of the board of directors of the Tennessee Valley Bank, serving several north Alabama counties. He also organized the First National Bank of Haleyville, where he served as president and one of his sons was hired as the assistant cashier. Another son, Oscar Pinkney (named after his mother's slain Curtis uncle) helped run his father's business interests spread across two or three counties. And the Drake Farm was acclaimed as an example of exemplary agriculture and a preferred site for local civic and charitable events. B. H.'s family now lived in one of the town's largest homes, and most of his children were married or soon would be.

MY GRANDMOTHER ANNA RETURNED with her two-year-old son to her parents' home in Littleville in early 1921. When B. H. Drake first met her is unknown, although it is likely he had known her since she was a child. Anna's father, Tom Steele, and B. H. were near the same age, and both came of age in Lawrence County. After their marriages, both lived in the same Gum Pond community, the section of Winston abutting Lawrence County. In 1897, Tom served as one of B. H.'s witnesses in a "final land proof," a document that permitted Drake to take ownership of one hundred and sixty acres of land around Gum Pond. As required by Abraham Lincoln's Homestead Act of 1862, Steele filed an affidavit verifying that Drake had lived on the land over the last five years and had made real improvements to the property. Soon after taking title to the virtually free land, Drake moved to Haleyville.

By the time Anna was eleven, her father had moved his family to Littleville on the Byler Road, where he farmed in the vicinity of the Drake Farm. When Anna returned home at the age of twenty-one, she was still child-like in physical appearance—especially in Drake's eyes since she was twenty-two years his junior—and younger than three of his eight children.

Whenever their romance began, by the end of 1922, B. H. Drake was uprooting his old life to begin anew. Throughout that year, he sold many business interests and turned over the operation of most of the rest to his thirty-year-old son, Oscar, now a locally recognized business and civic

Marriage certificate of B. H. Drake and Anna Mae Steele Suits.

leader. When B. H.'s twenty-year-old son, Russell, married Queenie Sue Flack in March 1923 in her hometown of Albertville, the *Birmingham Post-Herald*'s report of the wedding made no mention of B. H. and noted that the young couple would be living in Haleyville "with the groom's mother, Mrs. B. H. Drake"—not with the groom's two parents.

Less than a month later, on April 2, the Winston County circuit clerk entered the official chancery records of the divorce of B. H. Drake and "Molisie" [Melissa] Drake, granted due to "abandonment." For much of the nineteenth century, beginning with statehood in 1819, two-thirds of the members of the Alabama legislature had to approve any grant of divorce. But by 1923 Alabama law let circuit courts dissolve a marriage for six permissible reasons. Abandonment was one of the six, so long as there was a finding of "voluntary abandonment from bed and board for two years next preceding the filing of the bill." Therefore, if the law was followed, B. H. would have abandoned Melissa Drake no later than the spring of 1921, shortly after Anna's return to Winston County.

Two months after his divorce became final, county records verify that B. H. Drake married my grandmother Anna at her parents' home in a civil ceremony performed by Reylus Basiel Waldrop, Littleville's justice of the peace. The marriage of the county's prominent Republican businessman did not escape the notice of the Democratic editor of the *Winston Herald* in Double Springs. "A wedding of unusual interest was solemnized out on the Drake farm," the editor wrote on June 15. "The contracting parties being B. H. Drake and Mrs. Annie Mae Steele Suits. Mr. Drake is very popular in the financial and business world. He organized the Drake Mer Co., one of the most successful business enterprises here; he was also the promoter of the First National Bank, a successful institution; he numbers his friends by all who know him.

"Mrs. Drake is the daughter of Mr. and Mrs. Tom Steele," the editor continued, "and she is popular among her friends. We wish for them a long and happy life and may all their trouble be 'little ones.'" This last line echoes a portion of an old Irish wedding toast, but by the early 1900s it had taken on a more common, direct meaning in the United States, as playful postcards of the era illuminate. "May all your troubles be 'little

MAY ALL YOUR
TROUBLES
BE LITTLE ONES

MAY ALL YOUR TROUBLES BE "LITTLE ONES."

Postcards from the early 1900s.

ones'" often meant hearty congratulations on your newborn with best wishes for more to come!

Within weeks of his Littleville marriage, B. H. Drake began to leave behind most of his old life. He resigned as president of Haleyvilleʼs First National Bank and by the last half of July made it known that he had "purchased a large farm near Athens, Ala., and will very

probably dispose of his interests in Haleyville and make his future home at Athens," according to the *Birmingham Post-Herald*. The *Winston Herald* also reported that Drake spent several days in July and early August at the Elkmont Springs Lodge, a popular resort known in north Alabama for its restorative waters. It was located eighteen miles north of Athens slightly above the Alabama-Tennessee border.

Oscar Drake and one of his brothers-in-law, Obie D. Dodd, began doing business in Athens in the spring of 1923. They purchased at auction the merchandise of one of Athensʼ Jewish store owners, and Dodd moved there with his wife, B. H.ʼs daughter Effie, to run the new store. Shortly before Thanksgiving, "Mr. and Mrs. Oscar Drake moved . . . to Athens, Ala. last week . . . We regret to lose them, but Athens is the gainer," wrote the *Winston Herald's* Haleyville correspondent. "Mr. Drake has a large Mercantile business there."

The women in the Drake family apparently attempted to reconcile themselves to B. H.'s new ways, extending their work in the Baptist Church. While remaining with her mother in Haleyville, Ada Drake expanded her teaching of Sunday schools and Bible classes across Winston County, and B. H.'s other daughters and his ex-wife took on new responsibilities in the Haleyville church's community work.

By the end of 1923, B. H. Drake seemed to have cut all business ties to Haleyville. He sold much of his Drake Farms land in Littleville. He executed a promissory note as surety for all debts that might arise from loans his son Guy had made (surely on his father's approval) as a loan officer of Haleyville's First National Bank. He began liquidating Drake Mercantile Company, which publicly advertised its "Quitting Business" sale in the first weeks of 1924. His son Oscar returned to Haleyville during the Christmas holidays to manage the sale of one of his father's businesses and to visit his mother, family, and friends. The *Winston Herald's* special correspondent in Haleyville also reported in late December that "Mr. B. H. Drake of Athens is visiting friends and relatives here this week." The story failed to indicate which relatives. Was it the family of his divorced wife, Melissa Curtis Drake, or the family of his current wife, Anna Mae Steele Suits Drake? Or both?

Before the end of February 1924, B. H. showed signs of half-heartedness about abandoning his first wife. Oscar Drake returned his family to Haleyville after he and brother-in-law Obie Dodd took on new partners who started managing their Athens store, and by the end of that month, the *Haleyville Journal* reported that Ada Drake had spent the weekend "with her parents, B. H. Drake and wife, in this city." The Drake patriarch continued to live at least part-time in his large home on East Street in Athens. But Oscar and Odie returned from their brief residency in Athens and resumed expanding their family businesses in Haleyville.

No DOCUMENT EXPLAINS WHAT prompted B. H.'s change of heart in returning to Melissa. A family trauma occurred at the end of January when Guy and his wife lost a baby girl shortly after birth. B. H. also suffered from toxemia, a form of high blood pressure commonly found in pregnant women. His doctor had been monitoring his condition for years, and it is possible the occasional trips to the Elkmont Springs resort indicated that B. H. was experiencing an elevated condition. In any case, in late April he fell in Haleyville and cracked his femur. He was transferred to Birmingham's Baptist Hospital. By mid-May, when he had not fully recovered, Oscar, Guy, and B. H.'s daughter Cora rushed to Birmingham, alarmed that their father's condition was becoming critical. He was brought back to Haleyville but died on June 16, at age fifty-seven, in the home of his ex-wife.

His longtime physician, Charles Alonzo Olivet, said the cause of death was "exhaustion from neurasthenia," or what is commonly considered a nervous breakdown. This general diagnosis is not used in American medicine today but even in the early twentieth century it was rarely cited as the cause of death of men. Perhaps in combination with his high blood pressure, Drake had a stroke. His death certificate lists him as married and his wife as "Melissa" Drake, although no divorce decree involving his marriage with Anna nor any renewed marriage license with Melissa Drake exists in the Winston County courthouse.

"Shortly before noon Saturday, Mr. B. H. Drake, one of Haleyville's most highly respected citizens, died at the family home after a prolonged illness," wrote the *Haleyville Journal* editor. "He had been in declining health for several months but had borne his suffering with Christian fortitude and patience." After noting that Drake was a member of the Baptist church and was the town's pioneering merchant and businessman, the obituary assured readers that he was "a devoted husband and father, and a true friend."

The *Winston Herald's* obituary stuck to the facts of his funeral, observing that it was held at Haleyville First Baptist Church and listing both the honorary and active pallbearers, who included his doctor and local postmaster Frank M. Johnson Sr. It referred to Drake as an "indulgent father, a church man" who left behind "a wife, three sons, Oscar, Guy, and Russell Drake, four daughters: Mrs. O. D. Dodd. Mrs. B. B. Campbell, Miss Ada Drake and Madge Drake and several grandchildren." It diplomatically did not name the wife nor indicate that there had been two.

ALABAMA
Center for Health Statistics

CERTIFICATE OF DEATH

STATE OF ALABAMA—BUREAU OF VITAL STATISTICS
STATE BOARD OF HEALTH

File No. for State Register Only.

1 PLACE OF DEATH County _Winston_
Town or City of _Haleyville_ No. _____ St. _____, Ward _____

Registration District No. _67-5007_ Registered No. _2 8_

2 FULL NAME _Burrus Hartwell Drake_
(a) Residence, No. _Haleyville Ala_ St., _____ Ward _____

PERSONAL AND STATISTICAL PARTICULARS

3 SEX _Male_
4 COLOR OR RACE _White_
5 SINGLE, MARRIED, WIDOWED, OR DIVORCED _Married_
5a If married, widowed, or divorced HUSBAND of (or) WIFE of _Melissa Drake_
6 DATE OF BIRTH (month, day, and year) _Oct 12 1867_
7 AGE Years _57_ Months _8_ Days _21_

8 OCCUPATION OF DECEASED
(a) Trade, profession or particular kind of work _Merchant_
(b) General nature of industry, business, or establishment in which employed (or employer)
(c) Name of employer _None_

9 BIRTHPLACE (city or town) (State or country) _Bartow County Ga_
10 NAME OF FATHER _Hartwell Drake_
11 BIRTHPLACE OF FATHER (city or town) (State or country) _Norfolk Va_
12 MAIDEN NAME OF MOTHER _Emilie Lewis_
13 BIRTHPLACE OF MOTHER (city or country) (State or country) _Kansas Co Ala_

14 Informant (Address) _Haleyville Cemetery_
15 Filed _July 16 1924_ _J T Curtis_ Registrar

MEDICAL CERTIFICATE OF DEATH

16 DATE OF DEATH (month, day, and year) _June 14, 1924_

17 I HEREBY CERTIFY that I attended deceased from _1908_ to _June 14, 1924_, that I last saw h— alive on _June 1, 1924_ and that death occurred, on the date stated above, at _12_ m.
The CAUSE OF DEATH was as follows:
Exhaustion from neurasthenia
Baptist Hospital Birmingham
(duration) _16_ yrs. _____ mos. _____ ds.

CONTRIBUTORY (Secondary) _Broken Thigh & Pelvis_
(duration) _____ yrs. _1_ mos. _4_ ds.

18 Where was disease contracted if not at place of death?
Did an operation precede death? _No_ Date of _____
Was there an autopsy? _No_
What test confirmed diagnosis? _X Ray & Physical_

(Signed) _____ M.D.
(Address) _Haleyville Ala_

*State the DISEASE CAUSING DEATH, or in deaths from VIOLENT CAUSES, state (1) MEANS AND NATURE OF INJURY, and (2) whether ACCIDENTAL, SUICIDAL, or HOMICIDAL. (See reverse side for additional information.)

19 PLACE OF BURIAL, CREMATION, or REMOVAL _Haleyville Ala_ DATE OF BURIAL _6/15 1924_
20 UNDERTAKER _J R Dozier_ ADDRESS _Haleyville Ala_

B. H. Drake's Death Certificate.

Despite his extensive holdings and financial dealings, B. H. Drake died without a will—or at least none was presented to Probate Judge John B. Weaver, who appointed Oscar as administrator of his father's estate. As administrator, Oscar's first filing to probate the estate listed himself, his six siblings, and "Mrs. Melissa Drake, widow" as lawful heirs. None of the numerous documents and records involved in probating B. H. Drake's estate mentions the other Mrs. Drake—Anna Mae Steele Suits Drake— nor do the circuit court clerk's records indicate any divorce in Winston or Limestone counties involving her and Drake. Nor during these years was there any mention in any official record of the boy to whom Anna gave birth.

Heirs to B. H. Drake's Estate without Anna.

7

Mr. Suitts Appears

These discoveries about my grandmother Anna and B. H. Drake did not produce a smoking gun proving that he was my grandfather, but they offered clear and convincing circumstantial evidence. The documented timetable shows that Drake married my grandmother in the summer of 1923 after his divorce from his first wife was granted a couple of months earlier, in April 1923. The divorce decree means that B. H. abandoned his first wife's bed at least two years earlier, shortly after my grandmother Anna returned to Alabama.

Twenty years afterwards, my great-grandmother swore that my father's birth was on July 4, 1922. It is quite possible that after two decades and at the age of seventy-eight, she disremembered the exact year. There was no entry in a family Bible nor a real birth certificate to remind her of the exact year. Since she could not read or write, she could not have recorded or read the date on any piece of paper. So, it could have been 1923 instead of 1922. In that case the marriage of Drake and Anna would have been the customary "shotgun wedding" when a young woman's father forcefully insists that the man involved "do the right thing" before the impending birth of his child. The fact that the marriage took place at Tom Steele's family home and was performed by the local justice of the peace without others apparently in attendance fits this interpretation of the facts.

The newspaper story about my grandmother's marriage also supports this view. The article had a veiled reference as to how different the older groom's world was from that of the young bride's, but mentioning "little ones" in offering best wishes seems a not-too-subtle acknowledgement of what had caused this uncustomary marriage. This explanation appears even more likely considering how the phrase was often used during that specific era in welcoming newborns.

Even if my great-grandmother Malvina (known as "Vina" and in the family as "Granny Steele") accurately remembered my father's birth date as 1922, the available facts suggest that B. H. Drake was my father's father. If the romantic affair between B. H. and Anna began as late as November 1921, after her return home from Texas, she could have conceived my father around the first of November 1921, with his birth nine months later, July 4, 1922, as my great-grandmother averred decades later.

Under this possibility, the "shotgun marriage" of B. H. and Anna was postponed until his divorce from Melissa could be granted. In this scenario, Tom Steele's insistence that Drake do the right thing and marry his daughter, who had already given birth to their son, was postponed until his old friend's divorce was granted in April 1923. Otherwise, one of Haleyville's leading citizens would have committed bigamy, a felony that carried a sentence of two to six years of imprisonment under Alabama law in 1923. Also, it was not likely that the upright Probate Judge John B. Weaver would have knowingly certified B. H.'s second marriage without a divorce decree annulling his first marriage to Melissa. And had Drake risked bigamy, it is doubtful that it would have gone unnoticed by the county's Democratic newspaper editor, who seemed quite alert to Drake's second marriage.

There remains one other necessary consideration: Why did my great-grandmother deliberately lie and list my father's father as "Gilland Suitts"? The local notary taking her statement could have garbled Gillean's first name, and, unable to read, Granny Steele would not have seen the mistake. Certainly, "Gillean" and "Gilland" sound phonetically alike. But adding the extra "t" to my father's surname was hardly an accident. Granny knew Gillean was not the father of Troy. So, why put an extra "t" into Suits as his family name. And, most of all, why not name B. H. Drake as the father?

My great-grandmother may have been illiterate, but she was a smart survivor. She knew that both Gillean's family and the Drakes were wealthy, certainly in comparison to the Steeles, and those families wanted nothing

Tom and Vina Steele in the mid-1930s.

to do with Anna or her offspring, whom they had erased from their lives. Therefore, the safest posture for the Steele family was to go along with the pretense, especially since out-of-wedlock births, though widespread, were an embarrassment for most families and seldom were publicly acknowledged. My mother came to suspect as much in the late 1940s, after she married Troy. She mentioned that she had heard that Gillean's family owned a great deal of land around Pratt City, where a railroad depot was located. But after Troy asked his mother and grandmother about it, he warned Mom never, never to mention that subject again.

The Drakes' refusal to accept or recognize Anna's marriage to their patriarch demanded even more caution. They continued to be a prestigious family in Winston County and north Alabama. Like his father, Oscar Drake found ways to expand his own business interests and his political role. Two decades after B. H.'s death, Birmingham newspapers were referring to Oscar as a "wealthy cotton broker," and he became one of the state's most prominent Republicans, helping to nominate and then campaign for Dwight Eisenhower's election as president.

Granny Steele might not have known that B. H. died without a will or that by law her daughter was the rightful widow and a rightful heir to his estate. She was unable to read the newspaper notices or probate records that erroneously listed Melissa as B. H.'s lawful widow. But Granny surely knew that the Drake family did not—would not—recognize Anna as B. H.'s wife and widow. And even if Granny knew or suspected what her daughter was due by law, proving it would take lawyers, and poor farming families like the Steeles had no money or know-how to retain lawyers.

Also, by 1943, when she sworn an affidavit as to the date and paternity of my father's birth, my seventy-eight-year-old great-grandmother was a widow. Tom had died five years earlier. After 1938, she also had declining health, little income, and the burden of raising and providing for Anna's teenage children. Faced with this reality, it is likely Malvina Blackwell Steele decided it was best for her family to survive by her swearing in a public document that, in effect, no one in the Suits nor Drake families was the father of her grandson. It was instead, as my grandmother always repeated afterwards, a "Mr. Suitts."

BROTHERS SERVE—Pvt. Troy T. Suitts (top) and Pvt. Junior Suitts (below) are the sons of Mrs. Anna Wilson. Troy, who is stationed at Columbus, Miss., has been in Service since Oct. 27, 1942. Junior who is stationed at Camp Beale, Calif., entered the Service on April 25, 1942.

Suitts brothers, 1944.

Granny's affidavit was not the first public document mentioning a Mr. Suitts. Her grandson, Gillean LaFayette Jr., was the first when he registered for the draft in 1940. Starting a practice he continued the rest of his life, Anna's and Gillean's son had his name printed on the government form as "JUNIOR only SUITTS." (He was also illiterate and could write only his own name.) Junior also listed his place of birth as Winston County—not Ennis, Texas. Likewise, my father, Troy, listed his surname as "Suitts" when he registered for the draft in 1942—a year before Granny Steele filed her affidavit. Did the two young men adopt a common fictitious family name with two "t"s because they were told by their elders that they had the same father, "Gillian Suitts"? Or did the young men know they were creating a new family name for themselves with the cooperation and consent of their mother and grandmother? They never said, at least not to anyone alive today, and I will never know.

All I can know is that the first appearance of the Suitts family is found in the Army records of two brothers, Junior and Troy Suitts. It also was the surname that both claimed when in 1944 the Haleyville newspaper ran photographs of them in their uniforms above the cutline: "BROTHERS SERVE—Pvt. Troy T. Suitts (top) and Pvt. Junior Suitts (below)." By whatever family design or deception, the

Suitts family emerged into existence when the two young men were old enough to leave home and fight for their country.

From all I now know, I'd have to bet that Granny Steele hatched the name for her grandboys. She was the matriarch, beloved, obeyed, and followed by her family. She was by all accounts a woman who negotiated and endured the hardships and dangers of rural Alabama from the end of the Civil War through the end of the Korean War and beyond until she died in 1951 at eighty-six. With her own past and her instincts for survival, I can only believe she was wise enough to know when and how to shroud parts of her family's past, especially when it involved her gallivanting, foot-loose, and fancy-free daughter, Anna.

Granny Steele on her eighty-fourth birthday, 1947.

8

Things Others Would Forget

The deaths of the men who fathered Anna's two boys marked the beginning of the end of her philandering ways, but not before their passing presaged a withering of prestige, privilege, and honor among the Curtis and Drake families.

Not long after Gillean's death and Anna's return to Winston County, where Gillean had abandoned the grieving Ada Curtis Suits, Probate Judge John S. Curtis began creating serious troubles for himself and his family. He overextended his business interests after financing the construction of two new buildings in Haleyville. According to state auditors, Curtis started secretly pocketing funds owed to the county and using his office to provide favors in return for payoffs while refusing to open his books for an outside review.

As a result, in April 1922, a local grand jury indicted Judge Curtis, and afterwards the state's attorney general initiated an impeachment trial before the Alabama Supreme Court, which in June unanimously found him guilty of corruption and removed him from office.

Five months later, the impeached judge was arrested in Birmingham in the company of a fifteen-year-old schoolgirl, Grace Wright, a student attending a girl's boarding school in Boaz in northeast Alabama. Curtis was charged with contributing to the delinquency of a minor. Press reports suggested he knew the girl and her family in Double Springs and had helped finance her education. In Birmingham's juvenile court, the young girl testified that she received a letter at school signed "Papa" asking her to meet him in Birmingham to buy her whatever she wanted. The letter included ten dollars for the train ride. When Grace arrived in Birmingham, Curtis met her and suggested they lunch together. He took her to the Reliance Hotel opposite the terminal station, but instead of entering the hotel's restaurant, he took a room registering as "J. E. Curtis and daughter." Within minutes of their entering the room, two alert Birmingham police detectives knocked on the locked door. When Curtis opened it, he was arrested.

The policemen testified in court that Judge Curtis offered them $500 if they would permit him to go free. He admitted his "immoral purposes," but defended himself by besmirching the girl's "reputation for virtue." Curtis's Birmingham attorney was Clarence Mullins, who would become a federal district court judge twenty years later. Under cross-examination, Grace "made admissions of offenses against her virtue," as city newspapers gingerly reported. But Curtis did not testify on his own behalf, nor did his attorney refute the testimony by Grace and the detectives as to the facts surrounding the arrest. The juvenile court found Curtis guilty and sentenced him to twelve months of hard labor and a $100 fine, the maximum penalty under Alabama law. The Winston County native appealed the decision, posted a $2,000 bond, and returned to Double Springs to await a new trial in the Jefferson County circuit court in late January.

Judge Curtis's arrest and trial were covered closely by Birmingham's three daily newspapers, but the affair became a banner headline on page one on New Year's Day, 1923, when the *Birmingham Post* reported that "Ex-Judge Who Lured Girl to City Escapes With $100 Fine." In the lull of court business after Christmas, Curtis's attorney had approached an assistant district attorney who was uninvolved in the juvenile court case and showed him a letter from Grace's father, R. S. M. Wright. Wright asked that the case be "dismissed, stopped, and settled, as I do not want the disgrace and publicity" to continue. Based on the letter and the fact that "the offense was only an attempt"—in other words, Curtis did not actually seduce and have sex with the girl—the assistant district attorney approached Circuit Judge Harrington Heflin with a recommendation that the case settle with a plea of guilty, a $100 fine, and no jail time. Judge

Judge John S. Curtis in the headlines, 1923.

Heflin, the brother of Alabama's race-baiting US Senator "Cotton Tom" Heflin, signed an order approving the terms of the settlement.

"The Curtis case was a particularly heinous one," wrote the *Birmingham Post* editor. "Curtis is an elderly man, a former judge of Winston County who was impeached for misuse of county funds. His victim was a 15 year-old schoolgirl. Love letters which he had written the girl were introduced in court." The editorial called the plea deal "a gross miscarriage of justice." Faced with odious publicity, Judge Heflin charged that the assistant district attorney had misled him into thinking it was a "case of no importance" and directed that his order be rescinded and the case set for trial in his court.

The League of Women Voters (LWV) and a local "better citizens" group, the Law Enforcement League (formed to discourage vigilantism at a time when the Ku Klux Klan was gaining strength in Alabama) unanimously passed resolutions condemning the settlement. An LWV leader asserted that "such outrages as this make organizations take the law into their own hands." The newspapers also discovered that Grace's father had separated from his family and daughter six years earlier and, as the manager of the Haleyville Telephone Company, was a friend of Judge Curtis. Grace's mother and older sister wrote to the district attorney asking that he reinstate Curtis's original sentence.

A few members of the Birmingham local bar association joined Curtis's attorney in publicly defending the assistant district attorney's conduct, as did recently elected Montgomery Circuit Judge Walter B. Jones. In time, Jones's support would appear to be self-serving, since he would be arrested for molesting a boy at the Montgomery YMCA although in his case the arrest was covered up.

Despite what newspapers called a "shock to the public," Curtis's settlement was upheld by the state's higher courts. They ruled that a circuit court judgment in a criminal case, just like a jury verdict in favor of a defendant, becomes final once rendered into the official record. Revising a final order would constitute double jeopardy, a constitutional violation.

Throughout the controversy, Winston County's weekly newspapers remained largely silent about the affair. But in May, after the higher court ruling, the *Winston Herald* editor observed, "The many friends of Judge John S. Curtis are congratulating him on the successful outcome of his troubles with the Birmingham courts . . . and so closes the matter." The ruling did end the court proceedings but not Judge Curtis's other troubles in the following years.

In early 1928 Curtis ran to retake his post as Winston County's probate judge but lost badly in the Republican primary to the incumbent, John B. Weaver. Later that year Curtis was indicted by a federal grand jury for defrauding the First National Bank of Haleyville, although at trial he was found not guilty. Ten years later, the former judge was accused of fraudulently changing absentee ballots in a Republican primary. As the end of World War II neared six years later, Judge John Solomon Curtis died at the age of eighty-two in Double Springs. "Although advanced in years," the local obituary noted, "his memory remained excellent and . . . he could remember, without consulting records, details of thousands of property transfers." No doubt he also remembered things he had hoped others would forget.

Gravestone of former judge John S. Curtis.

As PUBLICITY OF JUDGE Curtis's troubles died down, those of the Drake family became complicated with the death of their patriarch in 1924. After B. H.'s oldest son became an administrator of his father's estate, Oscar failed to do anything to settle his father's estate for more than eighteen months. In June 1925, the First National Bank of Haleyville complained in a petition that the estate owed the bank more than $37,000, a debt that was past due, and that Oscar had failed to file an accounting or to satisfy the debt. Six months later, after negotiating with the bank, Oscar admitted in a court filing that the estate owed the bank more than $39,000. He told the probate court that the debt could be paid only by selling much of the property that B. H. Drake had owned. He asked for an order delaying a graduated schedule of payments to satisfy debts.

The size of this indebtedness startled a friend of the Drake family who had posted the surety bond enabling Oscar to serve as estate administrator. In April 1926, the friend withdrew the bond. The court records also show that eight wholesale companies filed claims seeking thousands of dollars for unpaid goods that had been supplied to Drake's businesses that Oscar had been running. When Oscar finally did file an accounting of the estate more than two years after his father's death, it showed that the estate's debts far exceeded the funds owed to the estate.

Oscar resigned as administrator, and the case transferred to circuit court, where an independent administrator of the estate followed stricter rules of procedures. During the next three years, B. H. Drake's land as well as store equipment was sold at auction to pay his personal debts. In 1928, Oscar Drake declared bankruptcy in one federal court and was indicted in another for defrauding the First National Bank of Haleyville. It was the same case in which Judge Curtis was indicted, and Drake also was exonerated at trial. During this same period, based on a procedural error, Oscar won a state court suit in which he was accused of avoiding paying personal debts to a creditor by switching the debts to his father's estate in a business deal involving his brother-in-law, B. B. Campbell. In June 1929, more than five years after he died from literally worrying himself to death, B. H. Drake's estate was finally settled. Few creditors were made whole.

Oscar Drake (1952).

Throughout this time, Drake's store remained open since B. H. had organized it in 1911 as a separate corporation which was not required by law to assume any of his personal debts. The problems and deceptions involved in settling his father's estate did not prevent Oscar from expanding his own businesses and becoming a major figure in the state Republican party. Owned by the Drake family and run by Oscar and later his son, the Drake Department Store continued as a major retail business in Haleyville for decades, and the Drake family remained during that time an integral part of Haleyville's civic life and the local First Baptist Church.

9

When That Name
Had Only One 'T'

In the months immediately following the death of B. H. Drake, my grandmother Anna's relationship with men appeared no less of a mystery. In November 1924, she gave birth to her third child, Olivia Christine, named with Granny Steele's middle name. All available records list the newborn's surname as "Cole," although her birth certificate is unavailable since Aunt Chris died in 2008 and her only son, Danny, preceded her in death. Remember: Alabama law bars access to a birth certificate to anyone other than immediate family for 125 years after birth. No marriage record of Anna and any man named Cole is in the courthouse of Winston County and surrounding counties. Years later, Aunt Chris listed on her first marriage certificate "Walker Cole" as her father. Only one man by that name is found in Alabama's records during this period. City directories listed a laborer with that name married to Minnie in Birmingham in 1920 and in Montgomery in 1930. But that was not the sort of man my grandmother sought or attracted. The manuscript census lists no adult male by that name in the nearby states of Tennessee and Mississippi in 1920 or 1930.

There were some Cole families in north Alabama, including one living in Double Springs, but none had a male adult named "Walker" nor any discernable connection to the Steeles of Littleville. There was a "Walter Cole" living in neighboring Lawrence County during this time. But he was married in 1909 and fathered two sons with his own wife during this period.

There was a W. B. Cole connected to the Drakes in Athens. William Baggerly Cole worked as a mercantile bookkeeper in Athens during the first two decades of the 1900s. Oscar Drake engaged Cole to manage the books of his Athens store after his father married Anna and moved there. In February 1924, Cole and another man became part owners of the Athens store. Is it possible that Anna met Cole and they became involved during this time? Nothing suggests such a liaison, but, based on surviving records, W. B. Cole was the only adult male of that surname who was likely to have had contact with Anna around the time my Aunt Chris was conceived.

It is just as possible that Anna and B. H. Drake conceived a second child in the first months of 1924, and Walker Cole was another fictitious character that the Steeles devised to hide baby Christine's true parentage. In either case, five months after Drake died, my grandmother gave birth to her only daughter, who, like Anna's two boys, probably had a fictitious surname to hide the identity of the father.

Grandmother Anna married again in 1930, six years after B. H. Drake's death. Her husband was Columbus Albertis (C. A.) Wilson, known as Bud, who grew up and lived all his life around the Littleville community. Wilson was a farmer and crossroads merchant. His first marriage in 1898 had produced three sons and two daughters. In April 1930, the census reported that C. A. Wilson was divorced. The first wife was in Michigan living with her married eighteen-year-old daughter and her family. The first wife reported to the census taker that she was a "widow."

Bud married Anna on August 16, 1930, in Franklin County where his brother's family lived. The marriage certificate lists her as "Mrs. Annie Mae Cole," which could explain why they were not wed at home in Winston County; local residents might have known that her latest surname was fictitious. The certificate shows it was Anna's third marriage—which also suggests there was no Mr. Cole since Gillean Suits and B. H. Drake would have been the prior husbands. And just like her other two husbands, Bud was much older than Anna. He was fifty-one and she was twenty-nine.

Nothing survives to indicate whether Anna's relationship with Bud began before or after he separated from his first wife or if it was the cause of that separation. What is known is that once the newlyweds returned

Anna and Bud Wilson (1930).

to Wilson's house in Littleville, none of his own children, one as young as twelve, and none of Anna's three children, ranging from ages five to twelve, lived with the couple or at any time afterwards. Her children—Junior, Troy, and Chris—stayed in the household of their grandparents and were raised by Granny and Grandpa Steele living down the road from the Wilsons.

For decades, Wilson took pride in demonstrating that he was a productive cotton farmer on his seven acres of land. Across the 1930s and '40s, he competed in the local newspaper's contest for who could grow the county's first flowering cotton bloom as well as the county's first boll of cotton fiber. In the years when he won, Bud often advertised in the paper that he was selling the same "Watkins beetle dust, fly spray, and stock dip" he used for growing his prize-winning crops.

AFTER ALMOST TEN YEARS of marriage to the same man, Grandmother Anna began gardening flowers as her primary pastime, and soon it became a passion. Over time the Wilsons' large front yard was entirely covered with sweet peas, saliva, petunia, periwinkles, verbenas, glads, irises, roses, lilies, tulips, scotch brooms, thrifts, poppies, phlox, sweet williams, snapdragons, larkspur, zinnias, and dahlias. Bud must have seen the garden as a business opportunity since he began advertising the sale of flowering plants. In 1945, his picture appeared in the *Haleyville Advertiser* "standing in his wife's pretty flower garden in the Littleville community on Haleyville Rt. 3." The photograph's caption added, "Mrs. Wilson raises some of the loveliest flowers." Twelve years later, they both appeared in a newspaper photo standing in her garden, each holding a bloom from "their yard of beautiful flowers."

Anna's three children grew into adulthood in their nearby grandparents' home. Tom Steele became a blind invalid in 1936 and died after a prolonged illness in 1938. The *Haleyville Advertiser-Journal* published a memorial by Anna about her daddy who "has gone from this world, but only to live with Jesus." She wrote that in facing "persecution and temptation" in life, everyone should "know that Heaven is waiting at the end of the way and just a little while all true soldiers of the Cross like daddy will go and share in the rapture that God has prepared for the redeemed. We will miss our daddy so much, but we know our loss is Heaven's gain."

Anna's boys continued to live with Granny Steele until both young men registered for the draft during World War II. In 1945, a month after the formal surrender of Japan, Troy reenlisted for a tour of duty in Korea. According to Army records, he returned to Winston County in the first months of 1947 and was united with my mother, still a high school junior, in a shotgun wedding in March. The marriage license listed Troy's father as

"Gillon Suitts," and barely more than a year later another marriage license for Junior listed his father as "J. N. Suitts." While the brothers differed as to their father's given name, both always claimed to be Mr. Suitts's sons.

Some old timers knew better. Not long after her wedding, my mother went to the Winston County Courthouse in Double Springs to pay overdue taxes for her husband. As she passed an elderly man who had heard her spell her married name at the office counter, he said, "I remember when that name had only one 't.'"

Granny Steele lived her last years with Junior and his wife, Earlene, and his sister, Chris, since Malvina suffered a stroke in 1946 and was mostly bedfast until she died in 1951. Her death certificate was signed by her attending physician, Dr. William K. Wilson, who in 1926 had married Lea Madge Drake, the daughter of B. H. Drake.

*Grandmother
Anna in
her garden
(1965), and
as depicted
in the
Haleyville
newspaper.*

Yard Of Pretty Flowers

Mrs. Anna Wilson of the Littleville Community near Haleyville is shown watering yard of pretty flowers, now in full bloom. Mrs. Wilson is renowned throughout this area for her variety and healthy growth of flowers. It has been her hobby for many years. — NWA Photo.

10

'Perished as Though They Had Never Been'

I have no memory of Granny Steele, only photographs of her in old age, since she died less than two years after my birth. My earliest memories of my grandmother Anna date back to the late 1950s and early 1960s when Mr. Wilson seemed to be waiting to die, sitting silently in a chair under a shady fig tree, and Junior's family (with two boys) lived next to her house. Mr. Wilson died in 1963. By that time grandmother seemed to have lost all interest in men but continued a few more years tending regularly to her acclaimed flower garden.

I recall grandmother was obsessed with the weather. It was as if she feared a dark cloud more than anything on earth. Near her house, the cracked, thin door of her primitive storm cellar opened into a small pit with dirt siding, a dirt floor, and makeshift, rough-hewn shelves holding a kerosene lamp and a few cans of unlabeled food. If a dark cloud appeared, Anna would fetch one of us grandchildren to accompany her to what she called her "storm pit," although most times not a single raindrop would fall before or after. My cousins Sherman and Mark, who lived next door, suffered through this year-round charade. Also, at their father's insistence, they often slept nights in Anna's house (in an unheated bedroom in the winter) because she was afraid to be in a dark house alone.

Grandmother had become manipulative, petty, and bitter about how her life turned out by the time I was old enough to notice her behavior. Adults called her "Anner," as if the soft vowel at the end of

Grandmother Anna's house—with storm pit behind—still stands in Needmore.

her name now needed a more guttural sound to match her personality. I remember that when I was about ten and visiting, grandmother always seemed to appear at Junior's house while Earlene was cooking supper. Often a melodrama unfolded. As Earlene finished cooking, she would call us to the table and usually tell grandmother that she had set her a plate too. Grandmother would reply that she surely didn't want to be a burden and knew Earlene didn't want her at the table. Then, she would pull a cup out of her apron, remarking "I'll just take a little something and be on my way" as she hurriedly spooned food from the table into the cup before rushing away.

Even as a child I knew that it was a bizarre scenario, but I did not learn until undertaking this family research the real back story. My cousin Mark told me:

> Grandmother was constantly at our house and was mean to Mom when no one was around. She complained if Mom didn't fix anything she wanted to eat and would tell her whatever she fixed wasn't good, always eating from a cup because our dishes had germs in them, she said. If anyone besides the immediate family was around, she would act as if she was the victim. She told Mom one year that she wanted a saucepan like Mom had

for Christmas. Mom bought her an identical one and grandmother threw it across the room saying, 'What did you buy me this for? I don't cook.'

Grandmother never cooked a meal. The only time she ever cooked for me was when she was paid to babysit me. [His mom, Earlene, had to work to make ends meet.] Grandmother always cooked instant mashed potatoes and chicken noodle soup from a can. She also made mom pay for that. Mom actually got upset because she would buy other easy things for me to eat and grandmother to cook, but grandmother wouldn't open the can and warm them. She would give them back and say she wasn't cooking them. Mom got upset when grandmother wanted more money for babysitting, and a sweet lady, Josie, kept me until I started to school.

As the youngest grandchild, Mark became my grandmother's frequent companion in the storm pit and her confidant as her aging memory continued to jumble together fact and fiction. Grandmother claimed Mr. Wilson owned the first Model T Ford in Alabama—perhaps confusing him with Gillean who was in the early automobile business. Each of her husbands liked to drink, she complained, and would get mean when drunk. Mr. Wilson, she recalled, was the only one she stood up to and would run him out of the house with a broom when he was drunk. She also confided that she would put a safety pin on her pillowcase to prevent her husbands from sleeping on it. Grandmother always remembered her husbands as a Mister—Mr. Suitts, Mr. Drake, Mr. Wilson—revealing by her terms of reference what she rarely mentioned in her remembrances—each husband was a much older man. Anna also claimed none of her husbands ever saw her naked.

Anna remembered she had outlived six husbands, including her last one, a Littleville widower named W. C. Goodwin, whom she married in the 1970s. When I asked why she married him, Grandmother replied, "All of you grandchildren grew up, and I needed someone to go to the storm pit with me."

Her count of six is telling. For certain she included Gillean Suits, B. H. Drake, C. A. Wilson, and W. C. Goodwin, all of whom were flesh and blood. But that is only four. To get to six, Mr. Cole and Mr. Suitts must be added to her memory list. It seems a proverbial case of a lie becoming a fact of memory, although she was accurate on one point about those two dubious husbands—they never saw her naked.

In 1984, when I interviewed Grandmother about her past with the man I thought was my grandfather, we sat in her cold, unkept house as she warmed to the occasion, showing real delight in my interest. Before we began, she asked if my wife, Ginny, and I would enjoy something to drink

or eat, although I knew she kept hardly anything in her kitchen. That afternoon she was full of gracious Southern hospitality, energy, and laughter, particularly when Ginny started photographing her as we talked. I felt as if I had glimpsed the young woman who had attracted those older men. I also left thinking that grandmother had loved the recognition and attention, and at eighty-six retained a good memory of her life with her first love. I was, of course, only half right.

AFTER SHE DIED IN 1990 in a Haleyville nursing home at the age of ninety, Grandmother was buried in the Littleville Cemetery which adjoins the old road that Gillean Suits regularly traveled when he met her. Close by, as the crow flies, is land

Grandmother Anna (1984).

Gravestones of Anna and Bud Wilson.

that was the Drake Farm. The cemetery has five generations of Steeles interred, including Anna's paternal grandfather and her parents. When I last visited, the entire graveyard looked different in my mind's eye. I saw for the first time that Malvina and Tom Steele's graves provide only their common names and with a caveat, "Dates Unknown." Anna's small gravestone lies twenty five yards from their markers, close to an even smaller stone with no dates for C. A. "Bud" Wilson. Her marker reads, "Anna Wilson Goodwin / Mar 26, 1899 / Jan 28, 1990." Mr. Goodwin's grave is on the grounds in another section. On the edge of the cemetery along a side road leading away from the Double Springs highway stand two large headstones, each proclaiming on one side, "Suitts." Buried there are Junior and Troy, the first two to live and die in Dixie by that name.

These graves would have been primary sources for documenting kin and clan as recently as thirty years ago before troves of census data, old newspapers, and other documents became digitized and often online. Along with a family Bible, the stones would have preserved the primary, lasting record for most family trees, identifying the dead and prescribing how they would mostly be remembered across generations. Amid these gravestones, I could not find Anna Mae Steele, the woman whose life choices shaped my surname and my existence. The person I discovered through modern means seemed virtually lost at this eternal site, hidden under the names of her last two husbands, distanced in name and space from her parents (and other kin who helped keep her secrets), and spurned in life and in death by the families of the other men with whom she had conceived their children.

Standing at Anna's gravestone, I vaguely remembered a portion of a quotation from Ecclesiasticus, a book found in the original version of the King James Bible, that James Agee put at the end of *Let Us Now Praise Famous Men*, his searing book portraying in the 1930s the everyday life and death of the South's plain white folk. I later looked up the exact lines:

And some there be which have no memorial; who perished, as though they had never been; and are become as though they had never been born; and their children after them.

In coming years, the extra "t" in Suitts will continue to befuddle people. But the real story of how I got my surname leaves me and perhaps others who carry the moniker with a tale too complicated to often rehearse—and too Southern ever to disown. The true story doesn't render a portrait of my grandmother that she would have sought, although she might have delighted in how it captures glimpses of her amorous early life, her deep, determined desires, and her flair for budding like an innocent flower when inducing older men to her. In the end, I think Anna would have preferred my choice to seek out and publish what became her story. She may have feared a dark cloud on earth, but I believe she might have feared even more being fully ignored and forgotten in death, no matter how the story finally remembers her.

Corrigendum

Malvina Christine Blackwell Steele (February 4, 1865 – March 17, 1951).

Genealogical Epilogue: Scalawag James Monroe Blackwell

Researching the story of my family's name wasn't very different from the historical research I have done for other books, but of course my choices about what to disclose and how to interpret my findings are both personal and professional. As a result, this book is partially a memoir in which I have selected hallmark events, experiences, and developments to explore a crucible in my family life.

This approach to genealogy avoids the customary cataloging of numerous "begets," "begats," and "begots." That practice may be a godsend for family Bibles and constructing family trees, but it is a sure-fire way to kill readers' interest in others' family history and perhaps even their own. But this type of thematic, hybrid memoir leaves out many people and events that help shape or define a family's history, traditions, contradictions, and joys.

In this instance, my Granny Steele's role in creating the surname I carry may have been influenced by her own experience growing up in Walker County. Her father—my great-great-grandfather, James Monroe Blackwell, was a remarkable, fascinating character who also confronted the need to change a name in the family. As an Alabamian loyal to the Union before, during, and after the Civil War, he was among Southerners once called scalawag—a "local leper of his community," according a widely held definition that lingered for generations after being coined in 1868 by a Tuscaloosa newspaper editor.

That Southern sentiment may help explain why the Blackwell family's published history and related papers, kept at Walker County's Jasper Public Library, has nothing more than a listing of his birth and death on a family tree. There are some inter-generational recollections about early land grants recorded on pigskins, but nothing about the scalawagging Blackwell past. And as I suspected, he was nowhere to be found in the biographical dictionaries of Alabamians published from the end of the Civil War into the twentieth century since those sketches most often included former slave-owning planters, former Confederate soldiers, pro-Confederate educators, Democratic office holders, and post-war industrialists.

In excavating James Monroe's life, I took advantage of many amazing online genealogical databases at Ancestry.com and FamilySearch.com. They make researching family histories so much easier than it was as recently as thirty years ago. Back then, I often had trouble finding the most basic information about anyone's history, but the best source was the US manuscript censuses, which were available only on microfilm and readable only on large microfilm readers. It meant going to a library, often only near the location of your ancestor, or traveling to a regional branch of the National Archives to review rolls of microfilm with no search capacity.

Back then, I'm sure I would have had considerable trouble tracking James Monroe Blackwell across the decades in census records alone. For example, in 1860 the census taker's obscure, cursive writing appears to list his name as "James McReawell" or "Reackenell." On my own, I would never have considered such a person to be the head of the Blackwell household. Today, the online digital databases have software that intuits the spelling of names, and even that grossly mangled entry showed up in my first search results on Ancestry.com for James Blackwell residing in Walker County in 1860. The emerging use of artificial intelligence will probably make finding ancestors even easier.* Today, anyone can search for billions

---

* Beware, not everything linked by the databases' intuitive software is accurate. For instance, others were named James or J. M. Blackwell during this period in Alabama and one fought for and died fighting for the Confederacy.

of records from home, office, or a local public library, many of which permit database searches without cost.

A lesser-known online resource I used is the HathiTrust Library, which makes available complete, searchable electronic copies of thousands of old publications and government documents that aren't yet on most genealogy sites. It is where I found a copy of J. R. Phillips's memoir, which added flesh and blood to Gillean Suits's ancestors.

As in other states, the Alabama Department of Archives and History offers online important records about the state's Civil War, but ADAH also still holds a treasure of undigitized, often essential records and documents that can be seen only by visiting the archives and receiving the assistance of its librarians and finding aids. (Digitizing documents is expensive.) I've spent so many hours over the years with different archival collections and old newspapers that I've developed allergies requiring me to wear COVID-like masks and gloves when examining them nowadays. Despite the inconvenience, I find it much more reminiscent of the past to see and carefully touch original documents than to look at digitized or microfilmed copies.

I found rare, invaluable self-published books on local families and local histories as well as undigitized local newspapers at the Jasper Public Library and the Winston County Genealogical Society. Like other local public libraries and volunteer historical organizations, they often make their unique materials available free-of-charge, and in some cases their librarians will identify and copy relevant local materials for a modest fee so that serious genealogical researchers might forego traveling long distances. (Still, donations are essential in keeping their doors open.)

In the end, I found the richest materials revealing the essential characteristics and character of my long-lost Blackwell relative in the records of the Southern Claims Commission, which the National Archives has preserved and Ancestry.com and others have now digitized online. But gaps will always remain. Discovering a full story of people in the South from four or more generations ago involves living with disappointments along with delights when trying to recover Southern ancestors who never held public office, never authored books, and never accumulated fortunes from slavery.* Even finding accurate places of burial, if not "begets" and "begots," can prove an insurmountable challenge.

I began by searching the manuscript census records at Ancestry.com where I established that James Monroe's father, Ambrose Blackwell, was in Elbert County, Georgia (northeast of Athens) where his son was christened in 1808 with the name of an American president, although it must have come from a contrarian's disposition. That year James Monroe failed miserably in his first attempt to become president in a bid against James Madison. During the War of 1812, Ambrose joined Georgia's state militia to fight for American independence as did his father, John, who served decades earlier as a captain in a Virginia unit of the Revolutionary Army.

Some local Blackwell histories suggest the family members settled as early as the late 1790s in the Native American lands that later became north Alabama, but the 1840 census is the first record locating the family's James Monroe in the area. Federal records of land purchases and taxes in 1847 offer the first evidence of his residence in Walker County, and the 1850 agricultural census documents that he had eighty acres of land, with only twenty-eight acres improved. His farm had one horse, two milk cows, two other cattle, ten sheep, and twenty-two pigs. The regular census listed his name, age, sex, and place of birth as well as those of his wife, Elizabeth, and their seven children. (He would eventually have more than a dozen children.)

The 1860 census provided similar information, including check marks indicating that his children between the ages of six and seventeen attended school. If so, schooling did not continue for all of his later children since his daughter Malvina Christine, my Granny Steele, born in 1865, was illiterate, unable to write her own name. James Monroe Blackwell had no slaves, although a younger half-brother in Georgia, Ambrose Jr., an attorney, owned slaves as early as 1850. Ambrose also was a delegate to the Democratic state convention that nominated Georgia's first Confederate governor.

---

* Those whose ancestors were enslaved face even greater obstacles since no census provides even the names of slaves, only listing how many a slaveowner claimed as his property.

James Monroe's own activities during the Civil War unfold in the unique records of the Southern Claims Commission, which was established in 1871 to compensate loyal Southerners who lost property in aid of the Union Army. I knew of the records from other historical research but had never searched them for my own relations. These documents place Blackwell's farm in 1865 less than five miles southwest of Jasper, the Walker County seat where Confederate troops were often bivouacked, according to state Civil War histories. Blackwell's younger brother, Davidson, is also found in the Commission papers as a loyal Union man who lived in the same vicinity, although he appears to have been far less outspoken than J. M., as James Monroe was known.

WALKER COUNTY WAS MORE loyal to the Confederacy than Winston County was. Without strong community support, Union sympathizers were easily identified, detained, and punished for what Confederate soldiers—and others—considered seditious acts. In a letter to Confederate Alabama's Governor A. B. Moore in July 1861, a Jasper doctor told of how a "vigilance committee tried a man in this county for uttering black republicanism sentiments, and from the proof did not feel authorized to hang him. But he was ridden on a rail by some young men"—paraded in the street straddling a fence rail—and given two days to leave the state.

Later in the same year, another letter to Governor Moore preserved at the Alabama Archives from a Walker County farmer tells how Confederate loyalists were dealing with local citizens who were "declaring themselves in favor of Lincoln's government." A few of the county's Union men were "chicked"—apparently meaning tarred and feathered like a chicken—by the Confederate vigilance committee or home guard, both self-appointed and undisciplined local groups. Many county residents wanted Southern traitors punished "in a summary way." The governor warned against lawless acts but assured both letter writers that the "laws against treason and sedition shall be faithfully executed if it takes the whole military." Moore agreed that "any acts or speech on the part of any citizen declaring himself in favor of the Lincoln Government, hoisting the United States flag, or . . . any other acts of like character . . . are . . . subject to a severe punishment."

And your petitioner avers that the aforesaid articles were his property. That the same, as he believes, *were taken and supplied for the use of the Army of the United States; and that no voucher, receipt, or other writing was given therefor, except as is shown in this petition.*

The premises considered, your petitioner therefore prays that he may be allowed the sum of *eight hundred and nine 50* dollars as compensation for said property *taken* as aforesaid for the use and benefit of the United States.

James M Blackwell
Petitioner.

LEWIS & FULLERTON,
Solicitors.

STATE OF *Alabama* }
COUNTY OF *Walker* } SS.

James M Blackwell being duly sworn, [each for himself] deposes, and says that he is [one of] the petitioner [s] named in the foregoing petition, and who signed the same; that the matters therein stated are true of deponent's own knowledge, except as to those matters which are stated on information and belief, and, as to those matters, he believes them to be true.

And deponent further says, that he did not voluntarily serve in the Confederate army or navy, either as an officer, soldier, or sailor, or in any other capacity, at any time during the late rebellion; that he never voluntarily furnished any stores, supplies or other material aid to said Confederate army or navy, or to the Confederate Government, or to any officer, department, or adherent of the same, in support thereof, and that he never voluntarily accepted or exercised the functions of any office whatsoever under, or yielded voluntary support to the said Confederate Government.

James M Blackwell
Petitioner.

Sworn to and subscribed before me at *Office* this *24* day of *July*, 187*1*.

Jno Brown Judge of Probate
~~Justice of the Peace~~

WITNESSES.

To prove my loyalty I rely upon—

Samuel B Gooner residing at *Jasper Ala*
William G Norris residing at " "
John Bothell residing at " "
residing at

The other matters I rely upon—

Elizabeth Blackwell residing at *Jasper Ala*
Lewissa Blackwell residing at " "
Boston P Blackwell residing at " "
residing at
residing at
residing at
residing at
residing at

My Post Office Address is *Jasper Ala*

My Counsel are Messrs. LEWIS & FULLERTON, whose post office address is Washington, D. C.

NOTE—Accompany each petition with a Power of Attorney and an application to take testimony.

Page from Blackwell Southern Claims Commission Petition.

According to the sworn affidavits of Blackwell's neighbors (found in the Commission papers), everyone in the county regarded him as a Union man or an "Old Tory," a term secessionists used to suggest he was betraying his new country as had Tory colonists who fought against American Independence. The Reverend Simeon A. Smith, the first pastor of the local New Prospect Baptist Church, remembered that J. M. was "threatened on several occasions" because of his outspoken beliefs, so much so that Smith "always expected him to be hung." John Boshell, whose brother Andrew Jackson Boshell secretly hid and fed men evading Confederate conscription, avowed that Blackwell was "warned to leave the county in twenty days or that they would hang him," but he continued to do "everything as far as his means and power would permit" in support of the US government.

William Norris, a local farmer who volunteered with the First Alabama Cavalry USA and recruited volunteers in Walker County during the War, vouched for Blackwell's loyalty to the Union cause and his assistance to Union soldiers. A neighboring farmer, Samuel Cooner, saw a written notice that Blackwell received "from Confederate authorities." It stated that J. M. "must change the name of his child that he had named Abraham Lincoln—and change his principles or leave the county."* All three men also affirmed in 1871 that Blackwell had favored "the reconstruction acts of Congress—and openly and boldly expressed himself in that way."

J. M.'s own sworn statement made no mention of the naming his son but affirmed how he had always been a Union man and had announced his intention to vote for Abraham Lincoln even before the War broke out. His family prevailed on him not to go to the polls in 1860, he recounted, in fear for his own safety. (It would have been a vain task in any event since no ballots in Alabama bore Lincoln's name.) Blackwell recounted how he took in a wounded Union soldier and afterwards guided him safely back to his regiment. He also confirmed he had been jailed in Jasper by Confederate soldiers who accused him of being a Union spy. On another occasion,

---

*   This entry caught the attention of Margaret Storey who mentions it in her seminal book, *Loyalty and Loss: Alabama's Unionists in the Civil War and Reconstruction* (Baton Rouge: Louisiana State University Press, 2005), 27.

Confederate authorities demanded he leave the county or face hanging for treason. Blackwell "sent word to just hang him, but it would not change his way of thinking."

Too old to enlist, J. M. confessed that two of his sons, Preston and Joshua, joined the Confederate Army against his wishes. The father said that he never contributed anything to them while they were in the Army and tried to persuade them to desert and enlist in the Union Army.

The census and military records available through Ancestry.com and its separate database of military records, Fold3.com, reveal that Preston was a private in L Company of the Alabama 56th Regiment of Volunteers. He may have been captured by Union troops in early 1865. J. M.'s petition to the Claims Commission mentions that Preston was "with the United State Army . . . on 29th of March 1865" near Birmingham when the son recognized his father's horses among the Union soldiers who had requisitioned animals and supplies from his father's farm the day before. For his military service, Preston received a Confederate pension from the State of Alabama until he died in 1903, after which his wife continued to receive a lesser widow's pension.

Joshua mustered as a Confederate soldier in September 1862 and became a sergeant in the Alabama Partisan Rangers. He was captured by Union troops in Kentucky but returned safely to Alabama, resettling for some reason in Winston County. After his father was granted compensation, Joshua sought an award from the Southern Claims Commission for

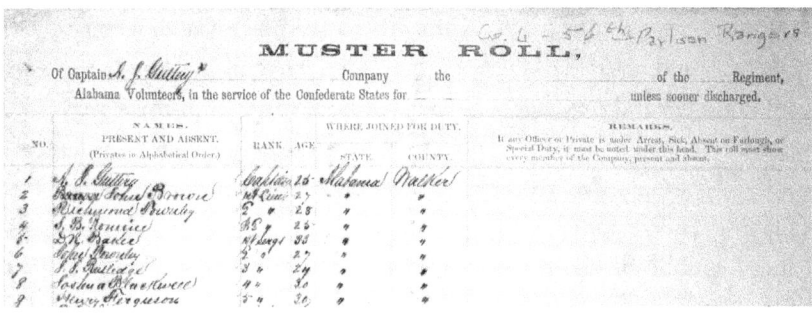

Joshua Blackwell on the Confederate Muster Roll.

supplies that Union troops took from his Walker County farm while he was at war.

Joshua's Washington attorney tried splitting some fine legalistic hairs to meet the law's mandate that only "those citizens who remained loyal adherents to the cause and the government of the United States during the war" were eligible. According to his petition with the Commission, Joshua "solemnly declares that . . . *his sympathies were constantly with the cause of the United States*; that he *never on his own free will and accord*, did anything . . . to injure said cause . . .was *at all times ready and willing, when called upon, or if called upon, to aid and assist the cause of the Union*."

His affidavit also falsely claimed he "did not *voluntarily serve* in the Confederate army . . . that he *never voluntarily furnished* any stores, supplies, or other material aid to said Confederate army . . . or yielded *voluntary support* to the said Confederate government."

It proved a vain deceit probably because US Army records showed Joshua had been captured as a rebel soldier. His claim was barred, as were many others who apparently had similar problems in documenting Union loyalties. More than twenty-two thousand Southerners sought more than sixty million dollars in compensation from the Commission, but its report to Congress shows that Southerners were awarded a total of only $4.6 million.

J. M. BLACKWELL WAS AMONG the very few compensated. He was awarded $593 as reimbursement for three horses, one hundred and seventy-five bushels of corn, and one thousand pounds of bacon, flour, salt, pork, and meal. They were requisitioned from his farm in late March 1865 by US General James Harrison Wilson's troops who lived off the supplies of Alabama farmers and merchants as they conquered much of the state in the wake of General Sherman's conquest of Atlanta and his march to the sea.

By the time J. M. received his compensation, Alabama politics was changing, and Republican Reconstruction in the state was in disarray. Alabama Republicans fractured, as some carpetbaggers and scalawags sought to create a "lily white" party by attacking whites and blacks who continued in the party's interracial wing. Whenever possible, Democrats accelerated defections by employing extra-legal methods against black and white Republicans. "They lost their jobs, got blackballed from business pursuits, were thrown in jail, placed into convict camps, threatened, and killed," according to historian Jefferson Cowie, who chronicled the demise of Alabama Reconstruction in Barbour County. By 1874, amid voter fraud and armed, local violence, including the murder of a scalawag election official, enough Republicans abandoned the party of the North and joined ex-Confederates to elect former Tory George Houston of Limestone County as Alabama's Democratic governor in what became the end of the state's Reconstruction.

Too little is known about this shift in Walker County because fires in 1877 and 1896 destroyed its courthouses and many of their records, including copies of local newspapers routinely preserved there. (Walker's courthouse was torched, often by arsonists, at least six times in the years between the Civil War and the New Deal.) Still, newspapers elsewhere in the state and later historical accounts provide an outline of the county's acrimonious transition.

In 1870, Walker County voted for almost all the Democratic candidates including its candidate for governor. In 1872, A. H. McClung, a former Confederate elected as a Democrat to the state board of education, reported on a political debate in Walker County. In the *Jacksonville Republican,* he disparaged Winston County's Republican Chris Sheats* for "offensive and indecent language" that he claimed caused many Democrats and Republicans to walk out in disgust, and the Democrat dismissed another Republican speaker as someone who had wandered in "from some negro hole."

In November 1875, with Democrats holding most state offices, Alabama went to the polls to decide on a new constitution that would in effect

---

* A schoolteacher, Chris Sheats represented Winston County in the state's secession convention of 1861 and was its most ardent anti-secessionist delegate. During the Civil War, he became a vocal advocate for "The Free State of Winston" and supported the Union cause. As a result, he was imprisoned for treason without trial by the Confederacy. During Reconstruction, he became an active Republican and served one term as a member of Congress after winning a statewide seat in 1872. He died a pauper in Decatur, Alabama, in 1904.

*Article on
expected
vote on 1875
Constitution
in Walker
County.*

JASPER, Walker county,
Nov. 1, 1875.
Editors Montgomery Advertiser :—
I have been making some speeches
in this county, but quit in disgust. It
is useless to try to argue men into
thinking as you think when they are
already of that opinion. Indications
show now that Walker county will
not cast a single vote against Constitution.
Very respectfully,   M.

reestablish white control of state government for decades to come. Shortly before the election, the *Montgomery Advertiser* included a dispatch from Walker County declaring that all Republicans had been routed so that the county "will not cast a single vote against the constitution." The prediction was close. Official returns show Walker County supported a new constitution by a vote of 659 with only 16 against. There is no way to know how Blackwell cast his vote, but, in light of his earlier political commitments and his nature, I think J. M. might have been among the lonely sixteen opposing the end of Reconstruction.

A surviving newspaper report encourages this conjecture. A year before the election, Blackwell's name appears in a roster of local officers of a regional unit of the Grange, a farmers' organization established above the Mason-Dixon Line that espoused fairly radical economic positions, such as co-op farming and fair labor standards, despite conservative Democrats also becoming prominent in the group in the South. If accurate, his role suggests J. M. may have continued to support ideas out of step with the state's prevailing political leadership.

Throughout these years, scalawags and old Civil War Tories such as Blackwell were singled out as pariahs across Alabama. In nearby Pickens County, the Democratic newspaper charged in 1870 that the South's scala-wags and the Northern carpetbaggers were guilty of "vile usurpation and villainous fraud" in politics. In the same year, a south Alabama newspaper charged that the "vile scalawags gloried" in the degradation of white people, and Tuscaloosa's *Independent Monitor* provided a ranking of Reconstruction's villains: "bad niggers, worse carpetbaggers, and worst scalawags."

Alabama historian Walter L. Fleming relied on many first-person accounts from this period to publish *Civil War and Reconstruction in Alabama*, the 1905 book that became the foundational history of Alabama Reconstruction for more than five decades. He quoted a Confederate colonel calling Tories "the most miserable, ignorant, poor, ragged devils I ever saw." Fleming summarized the prevailing consensus when he wrote that Tories were "as a rule, of the lowest class of the population . . . Secluded and ignorant . . . They were mercilessly ostracized and thoroughly despised by the Confederate element of the population at that time, and the same feeling of social contempt had descended to their children's children."

Fleming's quotation from the Confederate colonel became a favorite reference repeated for decades by other state historians, including William Stanley Hoole, who became director of libraries at the University of Alabama in Tuscaloosa. Hoole revered his great-grandfather, a Confederate officer killed in the Battle of Chickamauga, and embraced Fleming's assessment in *Alabama Tories*, a short book he wrote about the

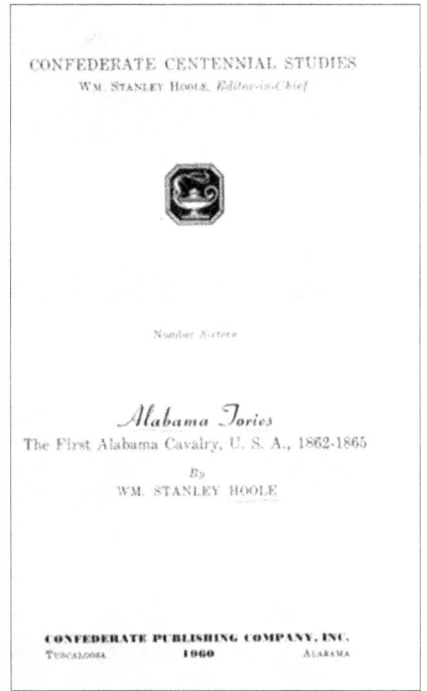

men who served in the First Alabama Cavalry USA. (Hoole also owned the Confederate Publishing Company which produced more than two dozen pamphlets and books on the Lost Cause.) While attending the University in 1967, I visited Hoole in his library office where I told him that I had discovered the existence of his book and was eager to read it since "I was born and raised in the Free State of Winston." He looked at me across his desk, paused, grimaced, and said, "How unfortunate for you."

DURING THE COLLAPSE OF Reconstruction, J. M. Blackwell surely realized that he and his family faced consequences far more dire than social contempt as he remained an unreformed old Tory, a scalawag who was among the very few in his community compensated by the Republican-controlled Claims Commission for losses inflicted by Lincoln's army. Perhaps that explains why J. M. and his wife, Elizabeth, changed the name of their son, Abraham Lincoln.

The 1870 census lists a nine-year-old boy in J. M.'s household as "Heyson." In 1871, when J. M. swore his affidavit before the local probate judge for submission to the Claims Commission, he made no mention of naming his son Abraham Lincoln. And ten years later the census shows no Abraham but instead a young man of nineteen named "Isham" in the Blackwell household. A crude tombstone for "Isham C. Blackwell" in Walker County's Old Bennett Cemetery records his birth date as 1861. Therefore, it appears that after naming his son at birth in honor of President Lincoln, J. M. and his wife failed to mention his given name ten years later to the census taker and by 1880, the boy born Abraham had become Isham.

Isham was not a Blackwell family name, and there is no clear reason why it was chosen. It bore no connection to the Lincoln family until the twentieth century when a grandson of the assassinated president was given that name. (I did locate through Ancestry.com a death certificate for an Abraham Lincoln Blackwell who was born in 1864 in Polk County, Tennessee, in the vicinity of Ducktown, where incidentally Gillean Suits's father and grandfather lived around the same time.) Ancestry.com states that the name Isham "carries the meaning of devoted or faithful" reflecting "strong virtues, embodying loyalty and dedication," although that connotation has Arabic origins.

The name was fairly common in the 1860s. One fanciful idea is that Isham could have been named for the Union soldier whom Blackwell and his family sheltered and led back safely to the Union lines. According to surviving military records, Isham or Isam Feltman was a private from north Alabama in the Union's First Alabama Cavalry who was hospitalized for unspecified reasons in the Spring of 1864.

My great-great-grandfather probably had good reasons for trying to protect his family and his youngest son years after the end of the War. Shortly after the 1875 election, three of the state's Democrat newspapers in south Alabama reported, "J. M. Blackwell is in jail in Jasper charged with perjury." There is no way to know why since court records were destroyed by fire. He could have been a witness in a civil or criminal matter where he was charged with false testimony, but it seems under the circumstances more likely the result of politics.

Soon after the South's surrender, Republicans controlled the local courts, and a grand jury indicted the former Confederate commander at Jasper for his role in the War. Now, was it the Democrats' turn? In the War's aftermath, a former state judge who became a leading Republican testified earlier before Congress that a "Union man is liable to be accused of anything . . . and although there is not the least foundation for the charge, an indictment is found against him, simply because he is a Union man."

Why else did the state's Democratic editors find Blackwell's arrest noteworthy? Back then, the *Alabama Code* provided that, whenever challenged, a voter could be charged with perjury if he failed to "fully answer" all questions by election officials about his qualifications to vote. Using the courts to try to punish the man who earlier was willing to be hanged instead of surrendering his political views would have been a relatively mild form of political action during a time when murder, violence, and physical intimidation were used to influence voting.

At this critical juncture I came to a dead end, with no further documentary sources or oral histories. I am left only to speculate without any facts to verify what motives and circumstances led to this incident and what happened as a result. Everywhere I looked there was no other mention of the arrest or aftermath. Worse, surviving sources tell nothing more of J. M. until his death four years later. Four Democratic newspapers in south Alabama reported in 1879 the death of "J. M. Blackwell of Walker County." It apparently occurred around April 24.

Excerpt from 1880 manuscript census listing Isham Blackwell.

A year after his death, Elizabeth Blackwell reported to the census taker in June 1880 that she was keeping a household including a nineteen-year-old son named "Isham," four daughters, including fifteen-year-old "Christeeny" (my Granny Steele), and two grandchildren on a farm with thirty acres of cultivated land and twenty acres of woodland in Walker County. According to his tombstone, Isham died the next year at age twenty. The cause of death is unknown.

Also, there is no available document identifying when Elizabeth died. I did find Christine's marriage certificate to Tom Steele in March 1885 in the Lawrence County archives, but it is unknown today as to whether her mother was alive to witness the wedding. (Most of the 1890 manuscript census, including pages for Alabama, were lost in a Washington fire in 1921.)

Similarly, as far as I know, there also is no existing record of where J. M. and his wife are buried, although the gravestones of millions of others, including his brother, Davidson, can be located through the "Find A Grave" website. Perhaps, J. M. and Elizabeth became estranged from their kin, but the community's censure of Blackwell seems just as likely a factor. A Walker County farmer told the Claims Commission in 1871 that any Old Tory would have been denied the "charity of a grave" among his own kin in the county, if the Confederacy had won the War. By 1879, the Confederates had won the peace in Alabama, and an unmarked, unknown grave seems a similar denial.

Looking back, I can imagine now what may have prompted my Granny Steele (Christeeny) to decide it was necessary to change the surnames of my father and his half-brother decades later. She had been old enough around 1880 to understand that her father and mother had changed her older brother's given name as a way to protect him from ostracism, retribution, or worse. It was something a teenager would never forget.

ALL THINGS CONSIDERED, EVEN if James Monroe Blackwell were not my ancestor, it seems today a misfortune for a white Alabamian who did not surrender his opposition to establishing the South as a separate, self-governing slave nation. But, as Howell Raines has written, burying the memory of white Southerners who bravely opposed the Confederacy was a long-standing enterprise among Southern and Northern historians until recent decades.[*]

On the plaza of the current Walker County courthouse stands a 1908 Confederate memorial where three granite-gray soldiers with different rank and postures look blankly into the distance while the monument's chiseled words leave no doubt as to its meaning:

> Furl that Banner!
> True, Tis Gory
> Yet Tis Wreathed Around with Glory
> And T'will Live in Song and Story
> Though Its Folds Are In the Dust

The Alabama Historical Commission's nearby plaque erected around twenty years ago explains that the Jasper chapter of the United Daughters of the Confederacy dedicated the monument "to honor the 1,900 soldiers who served from Walker County."

Today's online tools of genealogy easily reveal this claim as a canard. Military records from the near-comprehensive site Fold3.com show 851 Walker County men joined the Rebel army while 151 enlisted with the

---

[*]   Howell Raines, *Silent Cavalry* (New York: Crown, 2023).

Walker County Confederate Monument.

Yankee troops. But it did not take new technologies to reveal that a claim of 1,900 Confederate soldiers represents a wild exaggeration of the local devotion to the Lost Cause. Anyone after 1860 could have read that year's census report on population to find out that, as the Civil War commenced, Walker County had a total white male population of only 1,610 between the ages of fifteen and fifty.*

Little wonder that his erstwhile family and local community left James Monroe Blackwell and Elizabeth with almost "no memorial . . . perished as though they had never been." But Abraham Lincoln's leadership endured, and the original records of that time were preserved along with the Union itself, even if Lincoln's name in my family history did not. As a result, I have been able to reconstruct a different, short "song and story" about an ordinary white Southern farmer who showed extraordinary courage in standing up against death threats, arrest, and harassment from a rebel government and community that defiled him for supporting Lincoln's anti-slavery government. Hopefully, enabled by genealogy's newer technologies and the preservation of local libraries and historical organizations, many more such stories will emerge out of the records and histories of the Deep South where forgotten Southern liberals and their traditions can be reclaimed from the unlikeliest places, as the story of my own great-great-grandfather attests.   ❧

---

* Confederate conscription in 1862 applied to men eighteen to thirty-five and later extended to forty-five, although the many exemptions included state and local officials, teachers, postal workers, newspaper editors, and others.

Acknowledgments

Although she dropped out of high school when marrying my father, Mom was an avid, lifelong reader. After reading Eudora Welty's book, *Losing Battles,* upon my enthusiastic recommendation, she hesitated when I asked what she thought of it. "She is a very good writer who knows her subject," Mom finally said, "but I didn't learn much. I already knew those people. I grew up with them." It was a reaction that perhaps spoke more about my mom's life and her enduring character than Welty's acclaimed writing, but her comment has pricked me often into pondering what Southerners who know of my subjects can learn from my nonfiction writing, including this book.

Perhaps for this reason, the people who read the first draft of my manuscript were my only surviving Suitts cousin, Mark, who was also generous in providing some of his own honest recollections, and my two sons, David and Phillip. As the big brother, David took the role of encouraging me to think more deeply about the personal meaning of what my family research uncovered and to include those reflections as a part of the story. The next person to read the text was my long-time editor, Randall Williams, who is an unsung public intellectual in the state that once claimed to be the Heart of Dixie. Whatever this book's final worth, these readers' comments and responses markedly improved it in important, differing ways.

It takes a village to write and publish nonfiction, even family history. Foremost are the men and women who carefully preserve the sources of our history across the nation. This group includes those in both research libraries and local public libraries, archives (national, state, and local), local genealogical organizations, and historical associations. In this case, I am especially appreciative of the assistance I received from Ken Barr and his efficient colleagues in the reference division of the Alabama Department of Archives and History, led by its expert director, Steve Murray; Treva Hood and Peter Gossett of the Winston County Genealogical Society; April Davis, assistant archivist of the Limestone County Archives; Jennifer Cohron of the Carl Elliott Regional Library; and Wendy Hazle, Archivist of the Lawrence County Archives.

Transforming a manuscript into a book able to be read on paper or on a device (and even heard as audio) nowadays is no simple, easy task. In this process, as in the past, I am beholden to Randall Williams, editor of Black Belt Press and NewSouth Books, for his keen eye and knowledgeable guidance, and to his partner, Suzanne La Rosa, for friendship and her decades-long stewardship of the publishing process.

Every book of history depends on the work of others. To ease the reader's experience, I chose not to include endnotes for sources in this book, but I want to acknowledge how much I depended on Donald Dodd, who was perhaps the first historian not to let Winston County's true history become a permanent victim of the Lost Cause; Margret Storey who more than anyone brought the men of the First Alabama Cavalry USA back to life; Probate Judge John B. Weaver, perhaps Winston County's first historian; US Congressman Carl Elliott, whose five-volume *Annals of Northwest Alabama* helped preserve the history of north Alabama's hill country at a time when many did not think the area had much worth preserving; and more recently, Howell Raines, one of Alabama's great truth-tellers who has always known how to put the hay down where the goats can get at it.

Also, I am indebted to several people who have influenced this book through their example or their counsel as to how I might combine memory and memoir with oral histories and documentary research in exploring the history of a place through a first-person narrative. They include J. L. Chestnut, Francis Walter, Jack Drake, Cynthia Blakely, Lynn Walker Huntley, Howell Raines, Connie Curry, Paul Gaston, and Sophia Bracy Harris. In addition, some old friends endured the burden of listening over the years as I haphazardly reckoned with my family relations, family history, and the place where I was born and reared. Some, but not all, are still here to read my expression of gratitude. They are Peter Buttenwieser, Allen Tullos, Jean Ball, Ralph Knowles, Mike Mobbs, Jeff Carter, and Tom Dasher.

Above all, in every respect, this book is due to the presence and influence of the two most important women of my life—my mother, Wanda Epperson Suitts, and my wife, Ginny Looney. I miss both dearly, although they remain a constant in my life.

Index

A

African American x
Agee, James 62
agriculture, farming 8, 11, 20, 31, 42,
    52, 53, 67, 68, 70, 74, 78, 81
Alabama
        1875 constitution of 73
        courts of 33
        Department of Archives and His-
            tory 66, 68, 83
        Historical Commission of 79
        legislature of 33
        Supreme Court of 45
Alabama Code 77
Albertville, Alabama 33
alcoholism x, xii
American Legion x
Ancestry.com 25, 65, 66, 67, 71, 76
Annals of Northwest Alabama 83
Athens, Alabama viii, 34, 35, 52

B

Ball, Jean 84
Bamford, Alabama 12
Baptist Hospital (Birmingham) 36
Baptists 17, 30, 35, 36, 50, 70
Barbour County, Alabama 73
Barr, Ken 83
Bartow County, Georgia 28
Bear Creek, Alabama 10
Birmingham, Alabama viii, 11, 12, 13,
    14, 17, 18, 22, 36, 42, 45–48, 71
Birmingham Post 46, 47
Birmingham Post-Herald 23, 33, 34
Blackwell, Abraham Lincoln 5, 76.
    See Blackwell, Isham
Blackwell, Ambrose 67
Blackwell, Ambrose, Jr. 67

Blackwell, Davidson 68, 78
Blackwell, Elizabeth 76, 78
Blackwell, Isham 70, 76
Blackwell, James Monroe 64–81
Blackwell, John 67
Blackwell, Joshua 71–72
Blackwell, Preston 71
Blakely, Cynthia 83
Boaz, Alabama viii, 45
Boshell, Andrew Jackson 70
Boshell, John 70
Buckhorn Saloon 29
Burrus, Kisey Emeline 28
Burrus, Mary Melissa Curtis 29
Buttenwieser, Peter 84

C

Campbell, B. B. 49
Campbell, Mrs. B. B. 36
Carl Elliott Regional Library 83
carpetbaggers 72, 74, 75
Carter, Jeff 84
Cherokees 5
Chestnut, J. L. 83
Civil War ix, xii, 3–5, 6, 9, 10, 28–29,
    44, 64, 65, 66, 68–77, 81
Claims Commission 66, 68, 69, 71–72,
    76, 78
Cohron, Jennifer 83
Cole, Annie Mae. *See* Goodwin, Anna
    Mae Steele Suits Drake Wilson
Cole, Olivia Christine "Chris" 51, 52,
    53, 55, 73
Cole, "Walker" 51, 52, 59
Cole, William Baggerly 52
Confederates, Confederacy 5, 65,
    68–72, 73, 75, 78, 79–81
        6th Alabama Infantry 10
        19th Tennessee Infantry 10

Congdon Mines 8
Cooner, Samuel 70
Cowie, Jefferson 73
Curry, Connie 83
Curtis Building 19
Curtis cemetery 18
Curtis, John S. 5, 6, 7, 15, 24, 29–30, 45–49
Curtis, Pinkney "Pink" 5, 6, 29
Curtis, William Verpo 29

D

Dasher, Tom 84
Davis, April 83
Decatur, Alabama viii, 10, 73
Democrats 13, 33, 40, 65, 67, 73, 74, 77
divorce 14, 25, 33, 35, 36, 38, 39, 40, 52
Dodd, Donald 83
Dodd, Effie Drake (Mrs. O. D.) 34, 36
Dodd, Obie D. 34, 35
Dodson, Myrtle Suits. See Suits, Myrtle Hammonds
Dodson, S. E. 14
Double Springs, Alabama viii, 5, 13, 14, 15, 17, 18, 30, 45, 46, 48, 51, 55
    newspaper of 29, 33
Drake, Anna Mae. See Goodwin, Anna Mae Steele Suits Drake Wilson
Drake, B. H. (Burrus Hartwell) 26, 28–38, 39–44, 52, 59
Drake, Cora 36
Drake, Dr. Thomas 15
Drake Farm 30, 31, 33, 61
Drake, Guy 35, 36
Drake, Hartwell 28
Drake, Jack 83
Drake, James 28
Drake, Melissa Curtis 35, 36, 40
Drake Mercantile Company 30, 33, 35
Drake, Oscar 31, 34–38, 38, 42, 49–50, 52
Drake, Queenie Sue Flack 33
Drake, Russell 33, 36

Ducktown, Tennessee 8, 76

E

East Lake (Birmingham), Alabama 23
Elbert County, Georgia 67
Elizabeth 67, 76, 78, 81
Elkmont Springs Lodge 34
Elliott, Carl 83
Ennis, Texas 7, 20–23, 43
Epperson, Billy xi

F

Fairview Baptist Church 17
Feltman, Isham or Isam 76
First Alabama Cavalry 3, 4, 5, 10, 28, 70, 75, 77, 83
First National Bank of Haleyville 31, 33, 34, 35, 48, 49
Fleming, Walter L. 75
Florence, Alabama viii, xi, xii
Fold3.com 79
Fort Campbell, Kentucky xi
Franklin County, Alabama 52

G

Gaston, Paul 83
genealogy xii, 8, 25, 61, 64, 65, 66, 79, 81, 83
Georgia 8, 67
Germany, J. W. 21
Gibson, Don x, xi
Gillean, G. H. 23
Gillean, Paul Herbert 17
Goodwin, Anna Mae Steele Suits Drake Wilson 3–7, 8, 18, 20–23, 25, 26, 31–33, 35, 36, 38, 39–44, 45, 51–62
Goodwin, W. C. 59
Gossett, Peter 83
Grange, the 74
Granny Steele. See Steele, Malvina "Vina" Blackwell
"GTT"—Gone to Texas 7
Gum Pond, Alabama 29, 31

H

Haleyville Advertiser 54

Haleyville Advertiser-Journal 54
Haleyville, Alabama viii, ix–xi, 5, 9, 14, 17, 18, 19, 23, 26, 28–36, 40, 43, 45, 48, 50, 56, 60
Haleyville Church of Christ xi
Haleyville First Baptist Church 30, 36, 50
Haleyville Journal 35, 36
Haleyville Telephone Company 47
Harris, Sophia Bracy 83
HathiTrust Library 66
Hazle, Wendy 83
Heflin, Alabama 20
Heflin, "Cotton Tom" 47
Heflin, Harrington 46
Homestead Act of 1862 31
Hood, Treva 83
Hoole, William Stanley 75
Houston & Texas Central Railroad 7, 20
Hughes, Hartwell 28
Huntley, Lynn Walker 83

I

Independent Monitor (Tuscaloosa) 75
industrial, industrialists 11, 65

J

Jacksonville Republican 73
Jasper, Alabama viii, 14, 68, 70, 77, 79
Jasper Public Library 65, 66
Jefferson County, Alabama 12, 14, 46
Jewish 34
Johnson, Frank M., Sr. 36
Jones, Walter B. 47

K

Knowles, Ralph 84
Korea 44, 54
Ku Klux Klan 47

L

La Rosa, Suzanne 83
Law Enforcement League 47
Lawrence County, Alabama 28, 29, 31, 51, 78

Lawrence County Archives 83
League of Women Voters 47
Let Us Now Praise Famous Men 62
"lily white" party 72
Limestone County, Alabama 38, 73
Limestone County Archives 83
Lincoln, Abraham 5, 31, 68, 70, 76, 81
Littleville, Alabama viii, 5, 7, 18, 24, 30, 31, 33, 34, 35, 51, 52, 53, 54, 59, 60
Looney, Ginny 60, 84
Lost Cause 75, 81, 83

M

Madge Drake 36
Madison, James 67
Marion County, Alabama 10
Maryland 8
Mason-Dixon Line 3, 17, 74–75
Mississippi 14
Mobbs, Mike 84
Monroe, James 67
Montgomery Advertiser 74
Montgomery, Alabama 47
Montgomery YMCA 47
Moore, A. B. 68
Moore, A. W. 30
Mullins, Clarence 46
Murray, Steve 83

N

National Archives 65, 66
Native Americans 5, 67
Natural Bridge 19
Needmore, Alabama 5, 58
New Deal ix, 73
New Prospect Baptist Church 70
Norris, William 70
North Carolina 8, 28

O

Old Bennett Cemetery 76

P

Phillips, J. R. 8–10, 66
Pickwick Dam ix, x
Pike (Wanda's brother-in-law) xi

Pinkney, Oscar 31
Pratt City, Alabama 23, 42
Presbyterians 14

R

Racket Store 30
Raines, Howell 83
Reconstruction xii, 70, 72–76
Reliance Hotel 46
religion xi, 5, 35, 39, 61, 62
Republicans 5, 12, 29, 31, 33, 42, 48,
    50, 72–74, 76, 77
Revolutionary War 28, 67, 70
"ridden on a rail" 68

S

scalawags 64, 65, 73, 74, 76
segregationist 5
Selective Service Act 17
Shelby County, Alabama 12
Sherman Street, Ennis, Texas 20
Sherman. William Tecumseh 3, 22, 28,
    72
Shiloh Battlefield ix
Sipsey River 29
slavery 3, 65, 67, 79, 81
Smith, Simeon A. 70
Society, Winston County Genealogical
    66
Steele, Anna Mae. See Goodwin, Anna
    Mae Steele Suits Drake Wilson
Steele, Celie 5
Steele, Malvina "Vina" Blackwell xii, 5,
    26, 40–44, 51, 53, 54, 55, 57, 61, 63,
    64, 67, 78, 79
Steele, Richard Andrew 5
Steele, Tom 5, 31, 33, 39, 40, 41, 42,
    54, 61, 78
Steele, Wesley xii, 5, 6
Story, Fred L. 20
Suit, Huey 2, 13, 19
Suit or Suits, Gillean 2, 8, 10, 12–19,
    22, 59, 66, 76
    Suit, Gillean Huey 17, 22, 23
    Suits, Gillean Huey 11, 13, 16

Suits, Gillean Lafayette 6–7,
    20–25, 40–43, 45, 52, 60
Suits, Gillian 14, 43
Suit, T. L. 20–22
Suitts, Gilland 26, 40
Suit or Suits, Henry Huston "H. H."
    10, 13, 19, 22, 23, 76
Suits, Ada Curtis 2, 15, 16, 17, 19, 29,
    30, 35, 36, 45
Suits, Charles 2, 15, 17, 18
Suits, Gillean Lafayette, Jr. 2, 7, 21, 24.
    See also Suitts, Junior
Suits, Henry 8–9, 10, 76
Suits, Huston 2, 13, 19
Suits, Johnston 10
Suits, John W. 9–10, 11
Suits, Martha Jane 2, 15, 17, 18
Suits, Mary 9–10
Suits, Myrtle Hammonds 12, 13, 15,
    18, 19. See also Dodson, Myrtle Suits
Suits, Nancy Gillean "Tiny" 11, 15, 19
Suits, Ransom 10
Suits, Samuel 2
Suits, Steve 10
Suit, Thomas Lafayette 20
Suitts, Anna Mae. See Goodwin, Anna
    Mae Steele Suits Drake Wilson
Suitts, David 82
Suitts, Earlene 55, 58, 59
Suitts, Junior 43–44, 53, 55, 57, 58, 61
Suitts, Mark xii, 57, 58–59, 82
Suitts, Phillip 82
Suitts, Sherman xii, 57
Suitts, Tommy ix, ix–xi, 2, 25
Suitts, Troy T. ix–xiii, 2, 24–26, 27,
    39–44, 53, 54, 61
Suitts, Wanda Epperson ix–xiii, 82, 84

T

Tallapoosa, Georgia 20
Tennessee 8, 10, 21
Tennessee River xi, 10
Tennessee Valley 14
Tennessee Valley Bank 31
Texas 7, 18, 20, 21, 23, 24, 40, 43

Third Presbyterian Church of Birmingham 14
Tories 5, 28, 70, 73, 76, 78
Tullos, Allen 84
Tuscaloosa, Alabama 65, 75

U

Union Army 3, 10, 29, 68, 71
United Daughters of the Confederacy 79
US census 12, 13, 21, 51, 52, 61, 65, 67, 71, 76, 78, 81

V

vigilance committees 68
vigilantism 47
Virginia 67

W

Waldrop, Reylus Basiel 33
Walker County, Alabama 14, 51, 64–81
Walker County Confederate Monument 80

Walter, Francis 83
War of 1812 28, 67
Weaver, John B. 38, 40, 48, 83
whiskey 29
White County, Tennessee 18
Williams, Randall 82
Wilson, Anna Mae. *See* Goodwin, Anna Mae Steele Suits Drake Wilson
Wilson, Columbus Albertis (C. A.) "Bud" 52–54, 59, 61
Wilson, James Harrison 72
Wilson, Lea Madge Drake 55
Wilson, William K. 55
Winston County, Alabama x, 3–7, 9–11, 13–19, 26, 28–38, 42, 43, 45, 46, 47, 48–55, 57–60, 68, 71, 73, 83
Winston Herald 14, 17, 33, 34, 35, 36, 48
World War I 6, 17
World War II 26, 48, 54
Wright, Grace 45–47
Wright, R. S. M. 46

www.ingramcontent.com/pod-product-compliance
Lightning Source LLC
Chambersburg PA
CBHW071533120626
46550CB00006B/2441